**TANDEM**

The Tarot Speaks

The Tarot is popularly thought of as a fortunetelling instrument, but the initiate knows that that is but a side application.

As many could gain from knowing the Tarot, it is probably best to present it in familiar guise as the magic means of telling fortunes. Many people know me as a fortuneteller. Like the Tarot I have had to use this guise in order to teach, and in my case earn some daily bread, so I can say that this is quite a practical path to take towards learning its greater significance. Do not expect your fortunetelling skills to tell your own fortune, and be kind to the poor unfortunate victims who have the courage and kindness to let you practise on them.

If this book does not turn you into a fortuneteller, it should at least delightfully extend your horizons by giving your life extra purpose. And I think it can certainly be recommended as a consciousness-expanding experience.

RICHARD GARDNER

The Tarot Speaks

Richard Gardner

TANDEM
14 Gloucester Road, London SW7

First published in Great Britain by Rigel Press Ltd, 1971

Published by Universal-Tandem Publishing Co. Ltd, 1974

Copyright © Rigel Press Ltd 1971

Myths and the Bible have given birth to many pictures. These Tarot pictures have given birth to many words.

Made and printed in Great Britain by
Hunt Barnard Printing Ltd., Aylesbury, Bucks.

CONTENTS

ILLUSTRATION

Part One

Setting the Scene

THE TAROT is a work on the nature of the elements of our Cosmos in their finest energy form. Once we had split the atom we entered the world of energies. By having proved beyond doubt that everything in our universe is an energy manifestation, physics joined the world of metaphysics, which is a study of the nature of the energies lying behind all manifestations. It is clear to us now that ancient wisdom and the alchemists in particular knew more about these energies than we have known since the birth of our science. As alchemy was put down in favour of the chemistry to which it had given birth, many of the old masters bewailed the neglect of 'The Great Work' by the materialistic chemists. Indeed it was a great loss to us, and this is the time for going back to find out what we have forgotten.

The minor arcana of the Tarot symbolise the four elementary vibrations composing all manifestations. The major arcana go on to show us how to live in accord with their nature and what they are trying to do through us. A valuable work such as 'View Over Atlantis' by John Michell, points readers' minds towards gaining knowledge and power over the elements in physical matter. In this context the minor arcana becomes the tools of the magician to aid his concentration. For example if one can accurately perceive the energy elemental composition of any object; by concentration and manipulation one could change that object in all kinds of ways. Say the object had 4 vibrations of water, 2 of fire, 1 of air and 5 of earth. One would select the appropriate four cards by their number and type of symbols, and begin concentrating and manipulating. The symbol for each element is explained later.

One cannot become a magician unless one has control of consciousness and the ability to use its four main functions.* I have never met anyone able to do this to any effective extent, simple though it sounds. It is easy once one knows about these functions and practises them regularly. These four basic vibrations manifest in their finest form in the consciousness we use. It is this aspect of them that this book is about.

The next evolutionary step for us is to become aware of the consciousness that is manifesting through us, and with which we identify at present saying, 'I am like this. I never do that. I could not do something else' and so on. These phrases indicate that we have allowed certain elements of consciousness to dominate us, and have identified with them as if they were ourselves.

A great advance has been made when we realize that consciousness exists all around us, and that we either open or close ourselves to this or that aspect of it. Our true being grows upon how much we let in, digest, reconcile and express. Whatever positive performance we deny ourselves, we cut off a life giving charge that it contains. Therefore we age quicker than we need.

Two dynamics move us, and all that is around us. The vibrations water and fire, symbolized in the Tarot by cup and wand respectively. The mortar and pestle are the very

* For instruction in practising functions, see 'The Purpose of Love' by same author.

foundation of the Tarot as Yin and Yang are of the I Ching, which is another great work on the nature of elements, though perhaps a little too patriarchal to be used as the sole guide and philosophy for life.

All feminine religions of the past would have been rituals for growing consciousness in us activated by the blue energy essence of water. All the later masculine religions have been guided by the laws and attitudes which grow the dynamic fire element of consciousness in us. As these patriarchal religions have controlled our thinking for so long, most of our feminine qualities have now become subconscious. Our evolution towards individual greatness is achieved by using both dynamics and uniting them.

The two inert aspects of the energy (metaphysical) world, are Earth and Air. Both of these are moved and activated by the interaction of fire and water, and symbolized by pentacle and sword respectively. In order that we become whole we need to use all four aspects of creation in their conscious form. Therefore let us look at how they demonstrate their nature through our behaviour. We can then more easily see what we have developed or what we need to develop.

Our first great achievement was to grow the consciousness that derives from water (The Cup). This would have given us the following attributes:— Sensitivity to an enormous degree, even to actually feeling planetary influence upon us. Psychic vision of planets and stars. No need then for telescopes. This would account for astrology being born before the invention of such instruments and also why it fell into disrepute when we lost that degree of sensitivity. What we cannot experience we seldom believe. This remarkable sensitivity lead to our marking lines of the various planetary influences all over the ancient world, together with erecting 'power houses' at various points of particularly strong influence of one planet or another. There are a number of recent books describing many of these achievements, showing that we had a universal civilization of a totally different order and source of power from today. This consciousness in more recent times has been called imagination, psychic ability, even superstition. Lately it has been referred to as poetic truth, it is the process of associative thinking, and plays its part in the new phrase 'Lateral thinking'. Due to the declining grip of patriarchy it is slowly making its way through us again these days, although few 'scholars' have the courage to embrace it in their work. It contains all kinds of psychic skills, telepathy, precognition, ability to accurately picture past, present or future. To charm, to bewitch. To know by making a direct relationship with anything, as opposed to making a detached academic study of it. To hear: if you want to hear you must be still. To be able to listen and find joy in listening. All attributes related to receiving including Divine guidance. Its magic would impress us now as much as a television set would impress a bunch of aborigines on some forgotten isle. Being able to fly by natural means would have been just one of its accomplishments.

A study of Ancient Egyptian history reveals reports of one magical event after another, and this was at a time when the Golden age of water consciousness had floundered in the great flood. That is to say they were then living by just a small remains of an earlier great civilisation.

If you want to check your water consciousness ask yourself, or better still your friends. Are you receptive, can you listen, or only wait for others to stop talking in order to pounce in. Do you take your imagination as seriously as any other aspect of your being. Do you accept or contradict unfamiliar information. Do you take pleasure from learning more, or with thinking you know already? If your water is in a good state *anyone* can tell you *anything* without fear of your negative judgement. 'Facts' no longer constrict your thought processes when water flows. (The root meaning of fact is cognate with manufacture.) One is very broad and deep in water.

When the way of water came to an end with the flood, patriarchy was born and slowly over the centuries gave out all the laws and values that would, through time, begin to grow in us the skills of logic and will that this consciousness possesses. It is quick, penetrating, lively, spirited, has initiative, individuality. Defines and separates. Demands tension and quick reactions in the person it is in, and he will tend to demand the same from those around him. Ask yourself if you have these qualities, and can you also drop into the surrender of ego state that is water, and when the occasion demands can you be effective. Can you take definite action, show initiative. Are you free from fear of making an impression. Have you learned a skill or two, can you define things, be definite, can you show off, be witty?

The wand symbolizes the yellow vibration from the Sun which connects with the red fire of the earth bringing us skill and will. One can think of the emotional lady as a cauldron of water being boiled by the red fire of the earth. A sense of individual identity goes with fire often making the person impose his will upon others. Overdeveloped it is a tyrant telling you what way to press your toothpaste, tend your garden, paint your house and so on and so on. People who do this have no control of the red fire within them. It is obvious that one cannot be in a true state of water and fire at the same time, but it is essential for us to use both as occasion suits.

13

Most of us suffer from using only one type of consciousness for too much of our lives. No one need say; 'Oh I use both in proper proportion', unless he can prove he is a magician, for that is what would result from truly using both.

The sword symbolizes Air, controller of shape and form which is the element of our intellect. Almost the only element of our being with which 'education' concerns itself in this age. Air dominated people identify with knowing as opposed to doing, feeling or imagining. Detachment is its strong quality. On its own it is not bound by actualities. It lives in a world of ideas where one set of ideas is as valid as another, containing in itself no touchstone with which to test the real truth of anything. Very dominant in our time and its detachment has caused people to lose the way because they have forgotten the roots, origins and meaning of everything. Air controlled people usually think that origin sources and roots are but mere superstition, calling them so in the negative sense of that word. Criticism is another of its strong points, and that function becomes the negative biting wind of winter when the roots of the thing are forgotten. Its positive qualities are an ability to be formal, correct, precise, to have clarity, acquire academic learning, and be sufficiently detached to see clearly an event as it is free from one's subjective state. As with all elements it has its proper and important place, becoming negative, as do all the elements when developed at the expense of the other three.

The pentacle is the symbol of earth, which controls size and density and therefore the gravity of things. In us our girth and inner sense of security. We all know what an earthly person is like, slow, heavy, natural, instinctive, reliable, relentless, realistic, practical, down to earth. When overly earth developed, no time for theories, dense, crude and insolent. A great value of earth is relaxation and goingness, its acceptance and ability to put up with things, its sense of security irrespective of a person's material condition. Without it we are constantly tense and do not really know how it is in the world or how other people are. In itself it is free of separating ideas and allows us to experience one another in complete informality.

These then are the four basic functions which for our wellbeing and growth towards further evolution, we must keep alive in us all through our lives. Bear in mind there is a great difference between affecting to do something and really doing it. If we did truly practise all four functions our lives would become increasingly longer and younger on our way towards a great mutation—a mutation as great as passing from ape to man. All activities passive or active are taking energy in and putting it out, and in so doing we grow upon these energies. We age and die through what we are not doing and thereby deny ourselves various forms of revitalising energies. This rejuvenating phenomenon is nowhere more clearly seen than in sex change. Many must have observed how much younger, say a man of forty becomes if a sex change to a female occurs. I have often been amazed at the effect upon a man of middle years taking to wearing female garb. Even where his friends and wife know that it is him they cannot control their natural response to the clothes and behave towards him as if a woman. With the clothes and response to them the man is liberated to act like a woman, and in a matter of weeks, ten years have fallen away from the man's body and mind, very visible for all to see. One wonders was this the original idea behind pantomime where female roles are played by males and vice versa? Contrary to ignorant opinion this role changing in no way indicates latent homosexual drives seeking expression. In the cases of which I am aware the man's natural drive towards the female was unimpaired.

The point of the above example is to try to convey the extraordinary potency of elements provided that we *really* use them. A man really behaving like a female means that he is using more of the water element. See what Jesus says about being born again of water. It seems very relevant here.

From the foregoing it is obvious that we should provide a time and place to regularly practice and experience the elements. Most cults and ways one comes across do not want to do anything that could really change anybody. And one will go a long way to find a person who really wishes to change or has the courage to face the possibility of doing so. Hence the evolutionary process has no alternative but to smash up one static civilization after another until we learn to grow individually.

The different numbers of symbols on pip cards represent quantities of the respective energy vibrations to be found in any object. When applied to ourselves, how much of any function we have grown. In a fortunetelling spread, the basic elements involved in any human situation. The court cards represent the elemental essences of men, women, youths and children. With true elemental knowledge you can select the appropriate card for a person and effect him. The essence of all persons fall within the symbolism of the court cards. I will not give further details of how representative court cards can be accurately selected for this purpose, because not many of us have outgrown the temptation to harm others rather than help them. This is the one great block, the devil himself that prevents magic from glorifying our lives. Overcoming the temptation to put another down in order to put yourself 'up' would unlock the doors of the magic which is LIFE and allow us to partake of its wonders. In practice I find one needs a very wide view of a person's life before you know how to truly help him by magical means. I almost never voluntarily try, but rather try to allow some magic words through me that will release him from where he is stuck. It can be a grave error to magically give a person what he wants. He is seldom ready for it and would flounder if he got it.

The Tarot is popularly thought of as a fortunetelling instrument, but the initiate knows that that is but a side application like opening a random page of the Bible for that purpose. Though the Bible has managed to preserve its reputation rather better than the Tarot, which in symbolic form preserves and reveals the same great truths to those with the humility to be Divinely instructed.

As many could gain from knowing the Tarot, it is probably best to present it in familiar guise as the magic means of telling fortunes. Many people know me as a fortuneteller, like the Tarot I have had to use this guise in order to teach, and in my case earn some daily bread, so I can say that this is quite a practical path to take towards learning its greater significance. Do not expect your fortunetelling skills to tell your own fortune, and be kind to the poor unfortunate victims who have the courage and kindness to let you practice on them.

Opening up and contemplating a spread in the light of what you should know about elements, is rather like looking at a game of chess. It is said that there are two ways of playing chess successfully, the intellectual or the artistic. The first working out the logical progressive moves, their rules and increasing complications as you look ahead. The second, looking at the pattern as an artist sensing danger where the pattern is in discord, seeing the next move as a creative contribution to the pattern unfolding in your favour. This latter approach is the only one I am capable of using, and in one form or another is the way most fortunetellers who are any good at the job.

Whatever means we use to make involuntary patterns those patterns will tell us something about how we are, and from how we are comes which direction we are moving and what is going to happen to us. The opportunities we shall grasp, those we shall not recognize and let slip and so on. The inner talents we are exploiting, those we are allowing to remain dormant. Oh dear! when all this vibrating pattern lies out before me I sense for a second what it must be like for the inquirer. There is always so much or so little, almost every choice or decision in life has this awful aspect. And it is true, it is why we are afraid of living, settling for what we think is safe and letting so much else pass us by.

Well somewhere in that pattern before you is your client in some way shouting for help, THERE ARE NONE OF US WHO ARE NOT. You gaze upon the pattern seeking soul and inspiration for just that magic phrase that can release him from a constricting circumstance, sometimes the phrase comes. You write it down, he reads it, the magic works and he goes on to new experiences. All great and great for all concerned. What is trapping us is mostly in ourselves although we are usually the last to see it, like the proverbial husband of the unfaithful wife. Really well informed fortunetelling can do much to show a person how he is trapping himself, and also to assure him of the right motions he is going through to achieve the ends he has in mind. Unless you truly know about the nature of the elements and their actual and visible reality as portrayed in human performances, your advice could be of any real value by chance only. Without the knowledge of these realities our advice and opinion merely comes from the very elements that are dominating ourselves, giving forth that which suits them, not what suits the needs of another in his pattern. If you are the knight in chess it is no good advising the castle to follow in your footsteps.

It is this damned air in this century, grown out of all proportion that prevents people from really feeling how it is for another person, it knows life only by abstractions. To put air in its place we should not be allowed 'to know' about anything we cannot do and are not involved in. This would put an end to all that rubbish we get called theories, opinions, the image of a person instead of what that person really is, and we do all have something, however small, that is real. Not many, if any, know what it is in themselves, but it is there. Our true friends recognize it and sustain it by the degree of that recognition. Those jealous of us deliberately ignore it, and when speaking of us however sweetly, will affirm some secondary aspect of ourselves which they quite rightly sense, does nothing to aid our growth, or self realization. Some people are such past masters at this performance that you can use them as a kind of negative lens to find the spot of reality in another person, for that is the one thing they will not affirm. We all have our uses, and as we are we might as well use each other. The person who so adroitly avoids affirming the core of reality in another could be the leading light of his age had he but the wisdom to use his gift positively instead of negatively. I have not the gift of truly sensing the shape of an individual's essence of reality. If I had I would be the saviour of the age, but I can get close enough to know that it is there and needs certain patterns of experience in order to fulfill itself, and that more often than not, many of the experiences it needs are denied to it by the *mores* of our time, and also by the person himself being disinclined to do what is necessary for his real needs. This mustard seed of reality within us, whatever its shape, carries the absolute might of God in it and will affirm its way however many life times it takes, or how many civilizations have to be created or destroyed to fulfill its needs. Sooner now rather than later it will have its way at the expense of all human attempts to deny it. The doctrine of the major arcana does much to guide us in facilitating its journey.

If you continue to tell fortunes, study the Tarot and any other great work on the elements, all the above and much more will become clear and real to you. You will *know* something which is a very different state from having opinions and theories. People will not be able to deceive you, for their very performances will tell you what they are and what they are up to, irrespective of their position in life. I often wonder at the wasted energy people that I know expend trying to deceive me in one little way or another. It makes them so cheap, whereas they could be employing their energies to cultivate their real attributes.

While it is true that in lesser matters we block ourselves, in matters of truth we are blocked by others. One need only study history to see the truth of this statement. Again and again one comes across records of the unfortunate fate of most every individual whose discovery later transformed the world in some way.

From knowing can come growing, this takes time, so do not be whirled off into space by what you could have learned by reading up to here. You may now know something you did not know before. How you are and what elements you are using will decide what if anything you have learned. If you are heavily dominated by certain crystallized thought patterns, all this is likely to appear to you as mere rubbish. If air dominates you it will appear as a fascinating theory of the rather tiresome man who wrote it. If heavily earthbound you will not have read this far. If fire motivates you it will be 'Too deep for me'. If water 'Oh what a lot of effort the whole thing is' will be your reaction, although out of all types you would be the most likely to understand it. If integrated I leave you to your own reactions, reminding you that there is no valid knowing that does not lead to positive doing. This is where that tiresome matter of having to grow enters our field of activity. You should know that you can grow only by using the four basic functions. The first step is to be sure that you use all four. Few, if any, do this at present. You are not doing it either unless you possess very remarkable powers, powers that are considered improbable in this age. In what way you may grow by using the four functions of the universe will be decided by your inner spark of reality plus what you are aiming to achieve. Being really true to yourself will bring these two into harmony, taking you more quickly to your true fulfilment. As a fortuneteller my aim is to personify sufficiently the four elements so as to have command of them that I may free any inhibited elements in my clients, thereby turning on for him or her a more wonderful life. It is only occasionally and in small ways that I ever achieve this, but I see its possibilities as limitless.

When you pick up the Tarot to tell fortunes it is some world you enter!

Now to concentrate on a more direct approach to the skill of divination.

Part Two

Fortunetelling Through the Tarot

USING THE TAROT for divination (which means Divine guidance) is a practical way of learning its deeper secrets and miraculous doctrine. When religions were real, functional, and did something for us, oracles were usually based in our Temples. Since religion ceased to perform any function at all, fortunetelling, like lovemaking, has been officially ignored and banished into darkness. It has become largely a source of shame and pretending that one is really 'above' that sort of thing, although women have always remained wiser than men in these matters. With lovemaking and fortunetelling banished from our religious practices very little is now known about either. It seems that not even the idea that something real can be known about increasing the ecstasy of lovemaking survives in people. In my first two books it was more than strongly hinted that great transformative results can be obtained from lovemaking, but few hearts have been gladdened by the news. Has the spark that could love been completely put out by generations of anti-love religions?

The history of religion is also the history of drug taking to aid intuitive insight. Today this has been banished into the realms of criminality. The conspiracy against the release of the subconscious has been total. This makes the sustaining of fortunetelling skills very difficult indeed.

The three main functions we most need to serve our further development have been eliminated from the church, the very place where they should all be taught and practised.

I have never found fortunetelling easy, never felt really adequate to the task, and have been guilty of the occasional misinterpretation. I have always had the sensation of seeing only the tip of an iceberg, sensing that there was much more in the pattern that I was contemplating than I could find the clarity to express. It is doubtful, under present conditions, if any other person, wishing to become a reader of the Tarot, will find it easy. Without the ability to be truly receptive and to cultivate a creative imagination it will prove virtually an impossible task. The food for imagination is to be found in the old myths and fairy stories. You should read these in the true knowledge that they belong to another form of knowing and perceiving. It is this kind of knowing that makes the poet and fortuneteller. These functions were always combined in our ancient Bards. (See 'The White Goddess' by Robert Graves.)

You must allow the pattern of symbols in the spread to play upon your imagination until meanings and connections begin to filter through. The sensation is like a fairy story in course of being created.

It is said that Leonardo da Vinci used to gaze fascinated at the patterns created by men spitting on the wall of a bridge. It is this sort of innocent regard for patterns of any kind that makes the fortuneteller or the great artist. A great intellect or ability to be critical or 'sensible' is of little advantage in telling fortunes. The skill is in the ability to see what is there, without imposing your own conditioning. Our own perception is the source of the ability. This is a faculty apart from education and learning, in fact modern 'education' often destroys this faculty, so that a person who cannot string half-a-dozen words grammatically together can be a good fortuneteller. His or her basic perception has not been constrained by narrow inhuman intellectualism. Intellectualism is only safe when kept in harmony with real human feeling and its needs. A person who is totally unsympathetic to fortunetelling has an unbalanced mind and has allowed himself to be trapped into the straight-jacket of our time, cutting himself off from the underlying patterns of all existence which give his life its meaning. This scientific intellectualism is what G. B. Shaw so rightly called 'The superstition of the twentieth century'. Fortunately an increasing number of people are becoming aware of its inadequacy to serve real human development.

The student may find a number of different meanings ascribed to the cards in various other books on Tarot reading. He may have already learned a different set of meanings, particularly for the minor arcana. This will not matter, virtually any set of meanings work quite well if you stick to them. We may find some day an exact and incontrovertible meaning for each card but in the meantime they appear to do their best for us no matter what we use them to symbolize. With the major arcana there is much more agreement as to their meanings and we are probably not far from discovering their exact meanings.

As an experiment I have read a spread using the meanings for the cards that I usually employ. Then I turned up a list in a book which had a very different set of meanings ascribed. In using those without any reference to my habitual meanings I found that I could read the spread just as effectively. The only difference was that it showed other aspects of the client's life not dealt with by the first set of meanings I had used. It seems that the gods do their best to help us once we give them any chance at all.

The state of language is no better than the state of card meanings. At present any sound we make can mean anything by general agreement. As we pass through Europe we cross a series of invisible lines, and each time we do so people begin to make a whole set of different noises about everything. In this age we have forgotten the dramatic origins of our words, hence we have few words with real meaning and therefore carry little power to be effective. It is not surprising therefore to find that there are no incontrovertible meanings for cards. As far as the major arcana is concerned, it is probably the most exact and truthful set of symbols that exists at present.

The Tarot is based on the elements, as are all great works of wisdom that reveal the nature of life and consciousness.

FIRE, WATER, EARTH and AIR.

The wand is the symbol for fire, the cup for water, the pentacle for earth, and the sword for air. Fire and water are the dynamic elements of our universe, and earth and air are the inert, moved only by the interaction of the two dynamics. The magic wand symbolizes the energy of the sun striking the magic waters (cup) of the earth. This interaction brings the air of our atmosphere into existence and all life forms including ourselves and the patterns of our lives.

The cup and wand are the foundation of the whole doctrine of the Tarot, as Yin and Yang are of the I Ching. The mortar and pestle symbolize the interaction of energies which give rise to all creation and its transformations, past and to be. Also they represent the interaction between male and female that can transform all their qualities and achievements into love.

For fortunetelling we are concerned with the effects of

28

these subtle and dynamic vibrations upon our lives. The querant is asked to shuffle the pack in order to show us what kind of elements he is using, and in what degrees. This gives his body an opportunity to communicate. It is the body it seems, that does the selecting during the shuffling. The body has a taste centre that is quite aware of the elemental nature of the performances and experiences of the person. Much information is centred in our bodies, but we seldom give it a chance to manifest. Dr Jung found that people often dreamed symbolically of future events in their lives. Symbolism is the language of the subconscious, and the language the fortuneteller must know. Fortunetelling is an attempt to get in touch with that function in ourselves that knows more about us than our superficial consciousness. It is worth repeating that this deeper more perceptive knowing is related to taste and smell. It can 'taste' or 'smell' what is going on around it, the elements a person is using and the dominant elements of others in his environment, and where all these energy vibrations are likely to lead him. In very early times this receptive sense was much more highly developed in us, and it is worth remembering that astrology was born before the invention of telescopic instruments. This suggests that we could psychically see planets and 'taste' their influences upon us. Even today the subject of astrology is useless in the hands of one with no psychic ability. It is a subject which demands both psychic and intellectual powers. We live now in a very tasteless age, showing that our intuition has been well suppressed. People think nowadays that taste is merely a matter of intellectual opinion instead of realizing that it comes from a much deeper sense of what is appropriate.

The meaning of the phrase 'We get what we are' is quite clear and very true. The elements we are using bring certain experiences. Those we over use or abuse bring difficulties. Those we do not use put the aspects of life they effect beyond our reach. The really advanced fortune-teller is one who can truly advise what elements of his being a person should cultivate in order to gain his desires, or to achieve a fuller and more meaningful life.

Before starting a consultation it is as well to sort out all the cards in front of the querant. Lay them out in, say, five little stacks, not putting any two of a kind on top of one another and seeing that all are the right way up. While doing this, quiet is best, allowing a psychic communion to begin between you and the client. Some clients do not shuffle the cards very much, so it is quite good practice to shuffle the cards yourself after sorting them while giving your attention to the querant. Then hand him the pack to shuffle.

Taking the shuffled pack lay out a number of cards, dealing from the top, into one of the patterns suggested later. Where we see WANDS (Fire) the information will be about action, skill initiative, pushing life onward in some way.

The Ace of wands would show the start of some new venture.

2. The intellectual nature of the work. Work with head rather than hands.

3. The inclusion of a partner.

4. The gain from consolidation of the matter, also a win, or near the death card, an inheritance.

5. Good fortune with business and career matters. Help from fate.

6. Is the sign of talents, or their growth. Suggests harmony in one's affairs.

7. Indicates movement, change in matters of work or

profession. It is also the sign for the dissemination of knowledge such as teaching, writing or publishing.

8. The card of diplomacy, speech, talk, persuasion negative or positive depending on what it is near. Can recommend greater diplomacy in the handling of some person.

9. The sign for advice, by the cards around it one must feel if given or received by the querant and on what matter. There is always something expansive about nines, so its influence is likely to expand any context in which it appears.

10. There is usually something administrative, large and consolidated about tens. With wands it would indicate big business deals, being in a strong enough position to launch out in a new line. Contracts and similar settlements.

Page of wands. A boy, usually bright. A messenger.

Knight. Young man of bright ideas, usually of an active business-like nature.

Queen. A woman of a somewhat masculine way of being effective.

King. Active type of man orientated towards efficiency. With all court cards the true nature of the person they represent must be deducted from the context in which they appear in a spread.

CUPS, the symbols of water govern the feeling, sensing, imaginative aspects of our lives. The archetype of the ace of cups is really the Holy Grail, our cup of happiness filled. The degree to which this is realized depends, as usual, on the cards around it.

When the ace of cups and wands appear in the same spread, considerable power to achieve one's objective is indicated. When appearing side by side this power is increased. Any cards that lie between these two aces can suggest what the querant needs to do in order to get them together. It is when they are together that they drive us forward to success. They represent the male and female essences. Any time these can be truly integrated tremendous creative energy is released taking us onward in a great surge. When appearing near love affair cards they indicate great rewards from truly loving. When applying only to the individual, greater psychological integration is indicated for him or her. An inner marriage of his or her male and female aspects which leads to increased being.

Ace of Cups. One usually indicates beginnings, so the beginning of a love affair. A love letter or when well aspected, fulfilment.

2. Whereas Ones start matters Twos are carriers on, the working numbers. Two of cups therefore tends to mean work one likes, hobbies, pleasant pastimes, congenial employment.

3. Threes indicate coming together. Out of any two persons coming harmoniously together, a third force is born, hence 3 for partnerships. Cups governing emotional growth, 3 means a proposal, a love affair or any liaison which gives pleasure.

4. Fours tends to indicate reliability, so with cups it would tend to mean a reliable friend. A re-union with a loved one, or with other indications, such as near the Empress, a birth.

5. Fives are associated with unexpected benign intervention of the gods in human affairs, five of cups suggest a really strong love. This card greatly enhances any romance it falls near.

6. Six is associated with conflicts and their reconcilia-

tion, so that 6 of cups well aspected indicates harmonious living together, domestic happiness with one's love. This is never achieved without the give and take which allows both parties to grow in his and her own right with love to transmute their differences.

7. The number of movement, usually heralds a change of home.

8. Eights tend to indicate a giving out of some kind, so this card suggests a spending on home improvements. For the single, a sign of marriage when supported by other signs.

9. The expansive, indicates one's wishes, that which one needs to fulfill oneself. Its place in the spread will show to what degree this is realized.

10. The consolidation aspect of this number governs, in cups, such matters as property, house or houses, gaining of honour, fame and other matters related to self fulfilment by whatever means including love.

Page of cups. A female child, a small creature one loves, a pet.

Knight. The genuine affection of a person for the querant.

Queen. A more feminine type of lady who exercises her power in the subtle way of drawing people towards doing what she wants, often without them realizing it.

King. A kindly man, usually a dreamer.

PENTACLES are the symbols for the element earth, therefore govern earthly matters. The highest manifestation of earth has long been considered to be gold. It is a female element and is often demanded by her as a substitute for true adoration by an effective male.

Ace of Pentacles. Very well aspected could indicate holding the world in your hands, wielding great temporal power. More often it just means a journey, a business trip, or travel to see a friend.

2. Wages, money earned by one's work and efforts.

3. A partnership or similar liaison where money is an important consideration.

4. A gift, a win, a bonus, a rise in income, a favourable project.

5. The help of fate in one's financial affairs, business or professional undertakings, success.

6. Usually indicates entertainments. The entertainment world, or just that one will be entertaining more persons for reasons suggested by the spread.

7. The moving number. With pentacles it is almost the commercial traveller's card, indicating as it does, money from movement, travel. It can also mean a change in one's way of earning money.

8. The outgoing number stands for expenses, spending money, investment, extravagance, depending how it is aspected in the spread.

9. With its expansive influence it can indicate spending money on friends often as a form of self promotion. It is usually a favourable number meaning that at least one has enough to allow the indulgence.

10. Usually means matters concerning large amounts of money. How large is related to what the querant is accustomed to handling. It would not indicate anything like a pools win unless supported by other cards.

Page of pentacles. A female child or spendthrift youth.

Knight. A bank manager, or another such person in control of money.

Queen. An earthly easy going type of lady, or when supported by suitable cards in the spread, a woman of wealth. When involved in the world of finance she becomes dull, hard and unimaginative.

King. Same as above, but a man.

SWORDS are the symbol of air, and in so many lists of card meanings they are associated with the unpleasant. Air is the element of our intellect. Criticism and analysis are its destructive effects upon us and everything which lives. It seems that we should use it sparingly, relying more than we do upon our feelings, instincts, sensibilities and intuitions as guides to our lives, and for the recognition of what is true. Appreciation corrects the negative aspects of our intellect.

In the following I will list the conventional negative associations with swords, but the more ambitious fortune-teller can go on to study numerology and relate the meaning of numbers to the various quantities of our intellectual powers. In this way he can lend an extra dimension to his readings from the point of view of advising the client on his or her self development. Intellect is only safe when balanced with all our other functions. Otherwise it is a cold sharp withering wind, destroying everything by criticism and understanding nothing. The intellect is the greatest slayer of the Real – Madame Blavatsky.

The Ace of Swords is the sword of Damocles threatening whatever it is beside or above. Illness is its main significance.

2. The number of work indicates strain, often through overdoing it in some way. It shows strain about whatever matter it falls near.

3. The severing of partnerships. That which separates people. Divorce or parting of lovers. Some partings are

temporary, so do not tell a client he or she faces a divorce unless there are very real supporting signs.

4. Regrets, see what cards are beside it, to know what is or will be regretted.

5. Benign providence again at work, a narrow escape, danger averted. When it appears near success cards, it may be a warning not to let a chance slip by.

6. Indicates risk, the taking of risks. Its placing should show whether they succeed or fail.

7. Danger, hurt in movement, could be in any kind of travel or sport.

8. This outgoing number means loss. Note the context in which it appears to know what is lost.

9. Disappointment. The opposite of the wish card. Also serious quarrels that can have lasting effects, badly aspected one would not communicate with the person again.

10. The ultimate of the negative in the minor arcana. Ruin, tears, loss. The unfortunate end of a way of living. Loss of one's means of livelihood. Near Justice for instance, can mean prison.

Page of swords. Usually indicates an irritable inner state of a person. One who has not recovered from childhood sufferings. A troublesome child. A minor enemy or false friend.

Knight. Quarrelling or fighting. Where illness is suggested, a surgeon.

Queen. Domineering woman. One who feels neglected or misunderstood, or lonely.

King. A just, usually stern man, inclined to the intellectual. There is often a hint of loneliness about all sword bearing court cards.

It is obvious that the meanings of all cards are greatly

modified by those surrounding them in a spread, and that much of the skill in telling fortunes is correctly sensing what any symbol means in context. Just as letters of the alphabet have many different meanings depending on the words into which they have been arranged, so with the meanings of cards. Our words, many of which have several meanings, have to be arranged into proper sentences before they give a real message. The meanings of words are greatly altered depending upon what one is talking about and the syntax of the sentence. The same rules apply to the grouping of symbols such as Tarot cards. Frequent practice is the best way to acquire the skill of reading symbols in context.

Little of any value is gained by us without dedication to the task, and this applies to fortunetelling. Do not be discouraged, because where any activity involving the subconscious is concerned immediate results are quite common, therefore the merest amateur who still has to look up lists of card meanings while reading a spread, will often give a little message that is quite valid or useful. Memory is not the function that tells fortunes, but direct perception, such as how people 'felt' to you when you were a child.

In the middle ages we communicated far more by symbols than we do now. Shops, for instance, invariably used signs, not written names, so that in those days our minds would have been more practised in symbology than now. This is a considerable loss to our intuition which thinks and manifests in symbols, such as in our dreams, and day dreams sometimes. Socrates' comment is quite valid when he says 'Since people learned to read they have forgotten how to think'.

The major arcana, the fortunetelling meanings of which now follow, contain a teaching about the nature of life far superior to that taught by the Church. When the Tarot came into Europe some five hundred or more years ago, the Church ordered it to be burnt, for in those days the people were familiar with symbols and it would not have been long before they, instructed by the Tarot, could have effectively challenged the teaching and authority of the Church. The Church called the Tarot evil, the work of the devil. This has always been the method employed by ruling religions to put down rival cults or gods. It is worth bearing in mind that we still live in very primitive times in this respect today. Witchcraft for instance, which is the religion, ritual and worship of the Goddess rather than the God, is still called devil worship by the Church and other ignorant people who know no better, and have allowed themselves to be influenced by the opinions of others instead of seeing objectively for themselves.

Card 1. The Magician is demonstrating his skill, so the card indicates skill, passing an exam, a quick minded person, the start of a new career. He can also be an actor or advocate. Negatively he is a cunning trickster personifying Shakespeare's phrase 'Men were deceivers ever'.

Card 2. The Priestess represents the sleeping hidden aspect of our intuition. Hidden knowledge is her main significance, secrets, inner wisdom. The virgin un-awakened part of our minds, or on the rare occasion physical virginity. When appearing in a 'work context she can mean discovery or work with the mentally immature. Negatively she is underhanded, deceptive and devious.

Cards one and two are the archetypes of the ace of wands and cups respectively, so that much of what has been said about these aces appearing in the same spread applies to these two cards, though more powerfully in the sense of reaching higher achievement. In a work context, discovery, in love matters a super orgasm.

Card 3. The Empress represents fruition, anything coming to fruition. Be it on the farm, in the factory, in the arts or the result of any endeavour. She aids growth. Stands for motherhood or a motherly woman. The inquirer's mother. Added power or wellbeing to a woman. Negatively a rather too powerful woman restricting the growth of the querant.

Card 4. The Emperor represents consolidation of manhood. A man of being or power, promotion, honour, worldly knowledge. Father or father figure, one in authority. Negatively an egotistical power hungry intolerant man.

Card 5. The Hierophant, spiritual knowledge, one versed in metaphysics. A Church. Near a journey, a pilgrimage. Near marriage cards indicates a church ceremony. Negatively a very head centered patriarchal man. A self righteous hypocrite whose motives are self-centered and can be dangerous.

Card 6. The Lovers show Cupid at work. The main emphasis of this card is choice in the sense that something always has to be given up for love. Love demands sacrifice. Positively aspected, great love. Neutral, indecision. Negative, promiscuity and inability to make up one's mind, losing one's way.

Card 7. The Chariot, real progress is its main significance. Progress truly meaningful to the inquirer, also drive and energy. Negatively, ambitious greed, ruthless pushing onward with no consideration for the needs of others.

Card 8. The Balance. Stands for justice, the finding of greater balance in oneself. Harmony in life. A legal matter. Negatively, the practice of inhuman law at work inflicting suffering in ignorance of the true human motives involved. A legal matter from which one receives injustice.

Card 9. The Hermit, sign of wisdom, cautious and knowing. As the English suppress their emotions, in this country he often represents an obstacle, because his caution will not allow things to happen. He is the very opposite of lively. Positively real wisdom. Negatively the caution that prevents one from entering the stream of life, missed opportunities, retiring into oneself.

Card 10. The Wheel of Fortune is almost the exact opposite of card nine. It is having a go and winning. Taking no thought for the morrow, and well aspected leads to higher living standards. Neutral, ups and downs of fortune. Negative, sign of compulsive unlucky gambling.

Card 11. The Enchantress, the great sign of true feminine power that can wield the male by charming in any way she wants. For a woman an important advance in the world. For a man, a sign of him releasing more of his own feminine creative power, or when negatively aspected, some female influence in his life that is too strong for him. The sign of subconscious power over the conscious. Like all great powers it can elevate or destroy depending upon its application.

Card 12. The Hanged Man. The sign for truth, as the truth is invariably the opposite of popular convention, he hangs upside down. Anyone seeing the truth about any major matter will be told he has it the wrong way round, and if he insists he is usually crucified in one way or another. So in divination he stands for anxiety, persecution, or victimization. Few people find it easy to face the truth, so there is always something uncomfortable if not dangerous about this sign. As card 13 suggests. Positively it is seeing what is true. Negatively it is suffering.

Card 13. Death, signifies sudden endings or drastic alterations in one's life over which one has no control. The end of one way of life and the beginning of another. Can show that the inquirer is in a low suicidal state, although seldom indicates his real death. Sometimes will show the death of a friend or relative. It usually ends what it is beside, when positive, ends what is unpleasant, when negative, ends what is pleasant.

Card 14. Temperance. The symbol for time, its influence is to modify extremes. Often appears as an indication of duration in any matter, or if in front of an affair, can delay its start. Its effect is one of joining together, controlling, managing. Positively it is the great alchemist bringing harmony to matters and taking the inquirer along the path of the Divine Plan. Negatively wasting time and ignoring the imperative commands of life.

Card 15. The Devil, represents the stupidity, ignorance and fear that holds us back from going with the Divine Plan. He is in every way a block, and more especially on good feeling. In a spread he often stands for enemies deliberately trying to harm, rage or spite. When applied to the inquirer himself, a block on his emotional nature preventing him from loving and growing. The holding back of what is positive is the devil's function.

Card 16. The Lightning Struck Tower immediately follows the devil as 'God is not mocked'. Meaning that any project or civilization founded on the suppression of good feeling, sooner or later crashes. It is the symbol for what is ruined, collapsed or failed. Just note what it is beside, business, plans, a home etc.

Card 17. The Star of Hope is the opposite in meaning from the preceding card. Starting again after the collapse of the old. It is always promising and assuring of better times, unless badly aspected indicating false hopes. When appearing in the spread of one in the entertainment world, can mean stardom.

Card 18. The Moon, more often plays a negative role in fortunetelling unless near a very positive symbol such as the sun, in which case it would indicate the balanced growth of the inquirer. On its own it suggests delays, jealousies, deceptions or underhandedness.

Card 19. The Sun brings shining success to whatever it is near. When appearing near journeys, usually indicates visits to warm countries, holidays. When associated with cards of commerce and travel, successful business trips. Success is its main theme unless inhibited by negative cards in which case the querant is desiring success, but not going about it in the right way.

Card 20. Judgement, release is the main significance of this symbol, in the sense that 'the truth shall make you free'. When we can truly assess any condition we are freed from its oppression. In a spread it tends to show release from some negative condition, enthusiasm, liveliness, renewal of life energy. An exciting project.

Card 21. The World. In the doctrine of the Tarot it shows a state of Paradise with the world dancing happily in the centre of a halo of totally integrated elements of consciousness. She and we are now perfect and whole, through our having perfected ourselves in every aspect. In a spread it means distant travel, synthesis, great happiness, fame or special success.

Card 0. The Fool. It is the symbol representing God in the Tarot, so this card is the trump of all trumps. Therefore it has many meanings and plays many parts in a Tarot reading. In the world of men, God appears to be a fool. Jesus was regarded as a criminal lunatic threatening the tiny, narrow, self-important and blind world of men. He would be regarded in the same way today by all of us who have not the courage to face real living. In a Tarot spread, only the context in which the Fool appears can give any idea of its meanings, which vary from the greatest heights of joy to the worst kind of catastrophe. God can do anything. When appearing among business or worldly cards, it is likely to bring failure through the foolishness of the querant. Appearing near signs of the church, likely to bring the wrath of that institution upon the head of the querant. It can also appear as 'An act of God' bringing a swift death or end to some person or matter. Near love cards it can indicate the ecstasy of the super orgasm which can join two souls together, the state in which we can experience something of the higher nature of God. Skill and experience are necessary to truly assess this card in a spread and to sense the degree of its effect and importance in any context. Sometimes it can merely mean one is dealing with a rather silly querant.

Some Tarot readers ask clients to deliberately reverse a few cards while shuffling. I do not find this necessary as the quality and power of any symbol is suggested by the context. Should any card appear upside down its meaning is always weakened, if not completely reversed, again the context will suggest which.

Some books suggest very large spreads, I would not recommend these. The mind and intuition fairly boggle if one tries to do a really thorough interpretation of such a mass of meaningful symbols. Twenty-one cards is usually enough to have in any spread at a time. If one can truly read these, one is giving a very good and impressive performance.

The skilled use of the following spreads described, is sufficient to satisfy most demands made on an operator.

According to one's taste, it is best to start off a consultation with either the Pyramid or Horoscope spread. Having read which ever one you have chosen, return all cards to the pack, shuffle well and return them to the client to shuffle. Then proceed to lay out a second pattern, which again can be the choice of two, using either eighteen or fifteen cards. With eighteen lay them out in six little groups of three, starting this time from the top left hand side as shown in the diagram.

If using a fifteen card spread, start at the bottom right hand side and lay down three rows of five cards, one above the other.

To finish the consultation shuffle the whole pack again and splay them all out in a line face down, then invite the client to select seven cards at random and have him put them one on top of the other as he picks them. This keeps them in the order selected. When the seven are selected they should be laid down, by the operator, in a row starting from right to left.

The reading of a chosen three of the five described patterns can be regarded as a complete Tarot consultation at any one sitting. It will take not less than half an hour, and if one tries to do more than this for any one person the power seems to flag. Then the message already given begins to repeat itself in various forms, or one finds that one just cannot make sense of the patterns.

Using three different spreads is a great help in deciding the emphasis of the whole reading, because often some of the same cards keep reappearing, giving some idea of what really comes to pass, as opposed to what is mooted, or mere wishful thinking on the part of the client. Some people have stronger wish projections than their ability to realize them, so one must take precautions against merely playing back their wishes to them instead of giving some real information. The profession is full of pitfalls

44

that only one's development can cope with. For instance I have described a situation to an actor or actress, which later turned out to be a part they played in a film. With writers I have sometimes described a scene from a book they were writing or about to write, although in the cards it all looked as real as life. What one often sees is what is fundamentally real to the client, so that if he is going to be involved in a situation meaningful to his needs that is inclined to look very real. Certain plays or stories can be what the psychologists call re-stimulative experiences and therefore touch some deep unfulfilled wish, or very pleasant or unpleasant experience in his past. In which case the experiencing of certain plays and stories is very real indeed and show as reality in the cards.

Questions have ever been the way of invoking the oracle and beginners are well advised to give readings regarding one specific question at a time, rather than attempting a general reading. General readings can be very confusing and apparently contradictory until experience in associating cards has been gained. Have the querant ask one specific question, lay out one of the larger patterns and see what it seems to say. Then lay out seven as a check on the indications of the first pattern. When one has mastered this, one can go on to more general readings.

As an opening pattern I favour the pyramid spread. After sorting out the cards and having the client shuffle them, lay them out face down, taking them one after the other from the top of the pack.

Starting at the right hand side put down eight cards in a row, above it put down six, then four, two and ending with one at the top. (See diagram.) Then turn over the fifth card from the bottom right. Then counting it as one, count in progression to the next fifth card turn it and repeat the operation until it takes you to the top card. There will now be five cards face upwards. These tend to give a key to the whole spread so that one will have some idea of what it is going to 'talk' about. Note them and the general feeling they give. This provides one with a starting point. It can be confusing, especially with the pattern of a total stranger, to look at the whole straight away.

Many Tarot readers say that the top card shows the outcome of what is shown in the pattern as a whole. This is not always so, it can often show what is dominating and querant. When one has turned over the whole spread and considered its general message, one can then decide what role the top card is playing.

Another favoured lay out is the horoscope spread. After the usual shuffling place twelve cards in a circle in the order shown in the diagram and then put one in the centre. This centre one plays a similar role to the top card of a pyramid spread. The following is a list of meanings ascribed to the various twelve houses. Placing a card in each house should give some idea of what is happening in those departments of a person's life.

Position 1. Personal qualities, state of mind, effect of environment.

Position 2. What is happening with money possessions or trade.

Position 3. Family relations. All means of communication. Speech, letters, writing, transport, neighbours.

Position 4. Parents' residence. Seclusion. House property or mines. Mother in man's case, or father in woman's.

Position 5. Unmarried sex ties, children. Creativity, speculation, schools, education, theatres. Places of amusement. All sensual enjoyment.

Position 6. Health, climatic or other effects upon it. Servants or subordinates, employees. Pets, food, clothing and all physical comforts.

Position 7. Marriage, partnerships, close friends. Contracts agreements. Litigation. Open enemies. Husband of woman, wife of man.

Position 8. Death accidents, dissolution, loss. Wife or husband's wealth or possessions. Partner's property. Legacies. Mysticism.

Position 9. Study, mental pursuits or exploration. Religion, philosophy. Publications. Distant travel. Foreign affairs. Relatives by marriage.

Position 10. Career, ambitions, attainments, honours. Employer or superior. Business affairs. Government.

Position 11. Ideals, worthy causes, societies, friends, councillors, companions, society. Wishes and hopes. Financial affairs of employers or others in command of querant.

Position 12. Restriction, sorrow, illness, confinement, restraint, prison, exile. Secret enemies. Plots. Large animals.

The card in the centre is again the likely outcome of matters indicated in the circle, or a very dominant influence in the person's life.

From the number of different attributes in each house, the beginner will see the wisdom of using the spread to answer specific questions, to give him some idea of which meanings are applicable. As your intuition grows the task grows easier, but so long as you rely only on the head and memory, nothing very valuable can be received, and trying to do readings will always be an irksome task.

Having opened the reading with one or other of the foregoing patterns, it is as well to follow on with another spread to see how matters move. Pick up all the cards, shuffle them and hand back to the client for reshuffling. Then lay out one of the following patterns, either the eighteen or the fiteen card pattern. (See diagram.)

The eighteen are arranged in six little groups of three, starting at the top left. One and four tend to reveal the state of home conditions, two and five personal affairs, and three and six, friends and the likely outcome of ambitions.

Sometimes there shows a considerable conflict between what each pair of threes is indicating. This often reveals a person who is rather confused, has not clearly defined aims, and is therefore not going through the right motions to achieve his ends. One should be able to say something useful or helpful from the signs that would help him to get onto a more successful path. There is little that is fatalistically laid down in our lives. In general we get what we are! This means that the elements we are using yield their results. Those which we do not use deny to us large areas of life experience. Most of us go through life using the wrong elements at the wrong time, thereby never tasting many joys we could have known. There is nothing that cannot be improved by a little hard work on ourselves. If we can make a significant inner change, life soon changes around us. In effect when we read a fortune we are saying 'If you continue in your present way of being, this and this will happen to you, but if you make certain inner changes, different types of experience will become possible.'

When advising on inner changes be sure not to suggest activities beyond the person's potential, which means that you must have properly understood the symbols. It is useless if not dangerous, to advise a client in accord with what suits yourself or your outlook. One man's meat is another man's poison in these matters. Where caution may work for you, it may be the very cause of another's missed opportunities. One must be free from like and dislike to see the symbols clearly and advise for the benefit of the client. Some are too square and need to let go. Others not square enough and need to practise self discipline. Some need a dose of mescaline or smoke of hashish to get free. Others should not touch drugs and should dedicate themselves to an activity meaningful to them. In almost all cases it is the things that a person will not do that holds him up. The first effective step on the road to true growth is invariably doing something one has considered to be against one's nature, or something one has been conditioned against doing. We can only safely advise a client when we are working totally objectively from the symbols, free from what we *think* is right or wrong.

Another follow on spread is to lay out fifteen cards in three rows of five, one row above the other, starting at the lower right hand corner. (See diagram.) The bottom line is said to show the past, the middle line the present and the top line the future. Reading them vertically one can often see how the past is affecting the present and future. If so, one can mumble on about what one sees, as sometimes this helps a client to see himself better, and thereby gain greater control over his affairs.

The last operation is to put the whole pack face down and invite the client to select seven cards at random. Taking them from him put them down face up in the order in which they were selected, starting from the right so that one reads them right to left.

All kinds of things can happen with these last seven. If the querant has been really helped by the reading, promising signs invariably show, as if he had gained the information needed in order to go forward. Sometimes the power of the reading has spent itself and the seven will return to

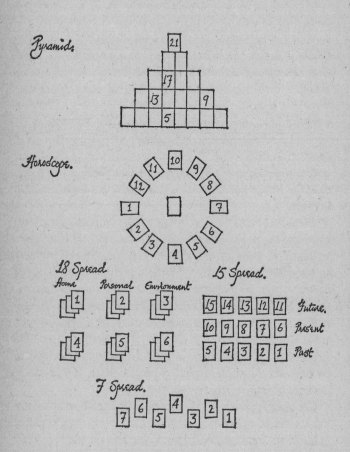

Pyramid.

Horoscope.

18 Spread

Home   Personal   Environment

15 Spread.

7 Spread.

some small mundane matter. Other times it merely sums up in 'shorthand' virtually the entire reading.

When consulting the seven on just one matter, the centre card tends to show how the querant is in relation to this matter. The fifth card, help he may receive, the sixth the unexpected or an obstacle, and the last, the outcome. For more information one can pair them, the first with the seventh, the second with the sixth, and the third with the fifth. So that with a favourable seventh the first card will indicate what helps towards this end. With an unfavourable outcome the first will give some idea of what is threatening the matter. The second card can yield more information about what is coming unexpectedly or the nature of the obstacle. The third card helps to elucidate the kind of help one can rely upon if the fifth card is favourable.

Two main conflicting hazards face the beginner, or even the experienced operator for that matter. Fortune-telling is an attempt to contact the causal world. We live in the mundane world of effects where we tend to think in very narrow 'logical' and not very imaginative or expansive ways concerning the realization of our greater potentials. The causal world is larger than life, so that when one looks at a pattern all is often exaggerated. The tragedies look far worse, the joys over ecstatic and so on, so that one must be careful not to mislead the client in matters of degree in any aspect of his life.

Conversely, there is invariably a larger pattern of possibility around us than we are fulfilling, so a person's spread is likely to show some of this. (And we should say what we can to help him expand into the greater possibilities.) In some cases it will be strong wish projection, in others it will be within his grasp if you can truly say how he may inwardly change in order to realize his greater potential.

I see this as the really important service that fortunetelling can provide, but it does take considerable experience or a very good intuition to do it, and even then, not for everyone every time. We all tune into some people better than others, and many people have not a sufficient spark of life or vision to see the importance of work on themselves. Advising on potential is the area where psycho-therapy and fortunetelling meet, as Dr. C. Jung discovered.

These then are the two opposing hazards, on the one hand the need often to play down the message, and on the other to see the greater possibilities and to help the person to realize them.

For successful fortunetelling the client needs to be in a very open state, so beware what you affirm, because there is a spot in ourselves that can control all. Should you inadvertently touch this it is likely to carry out what you say. Therefore go lightly and helpfully about what is negative, accentuating strongly what is positive in the pattern. By this means the client will be helped to draw upon his own inner strength and succeed. This omnipotent centre is what science is trying to reach with the idea of setting it in motion to grow another arm on a person who has lost one, and to perform many similar 'miraculous' activities.

May I wish you the best of luck with your soothsaying.

Part Three

The Tarot Speaks

FORTUNETELLING is to enter the world of magic. Magic is always around us, but we do not realize it. Fortunetelling brings that realization ever closer.

It has been a mystery to me since childhood, why the Church calls itself Christian while denying virtually everything of any importance in The Four Gospels. Jesus was a Master Magician and any society of Witches or Wizards would be proud to have Him and award Him the order of merit first class, yet not only has the Church refrained from teaching or practising magic, but has cruelly slaughtered millions of people down the centuries that it even suspected of practising it. Jesus said quite clearly that we would come to do greater things than even He had done.

In Fortunetelling we are concerned with what *is*, what is true. It is not possible to see what is true while we are calling something that which it is not, and saying that what belongs to it does not belong to it. Therefore it is all important to realize that we have been misguided from the top for centuries, preventing us from seeing our way and causing us to mistrust our own feelings, intuitions and ideas.

I am not writing this in order to take a crack at the Church, but to free the fortuneteller to see the truth. The Church is disintegrating anyway and needs no push from me to completely crash, and for the sake of truth God speed the day!

The new age will be based on the true magic of life and I seek to prepare people for this in any way I can. When the patriarchal yardstick breaks, many will be in danger of floundering if not prepared for this dynamic way of living.

In my last book 'The Purpose of Love' I gave instructions in how to practise 12 simple functions. Any group following these properly and regularly will develop magical powers far quicker than they would imagine.

Now to pass on to the doctrine of the major arcana.

ENGLISH TITLE:
THE MAGICIAN

ITALIAN TITLE:
IL BAGATTELLIERE

I am the Magician born on the yellow dynamic wings of the Sun, hastening to earth with skills of many kinds for men's aspiring minds. My hat bears the double elipse of immortality, and the shape of space time. Without me none may be truly male. I often rush through the minds of youths making them think they know everything and can do everything, but not until they can Do, is any portion of me consolidated in them.

Here on the table before me are the four elements, I can manipulate any of them. Many many skills are mine to give depending upon the kind of person who reaches for me. Disciplined and dedicated efforts consolidate me in man. He can then demonstrate some aspect of my skills to prove his fitness to be welcomed into the world of men, be it dancing, mathematics, music oratory or tumbling. All dexterous skills are mine to give, and all who receive them are transformed.

You should help all young men to gain me and recognize them when they have done so. Call them men for they have taken the first great step towards the dynamic of life that can make them male. It is not easy to be male, the source of that power is far from earth, so help your young males, for my gifts are great and all are well rewarded by efforts made to gain me.

You do not know all my skills or their meaning so do not insist that youth gains only those you think will pay, or are fashionable at any time. Put no limits upon me for I am one essential half of your chances of real immortality. If you would grow to perfection deny no positive expression then I can instruct you through many people with skills you have never seen, completely forgotten, or would not now believe. It is only people of very limited evolution who deny, and every denial is a denial of life.

There is no good life for man without me. He will have a mumbling, grumbling ineffectual and resentful existence. Bringing no light to the earth, no great joy or inspiration to the female, merely making her pregnant instead of awakening her consciousness that awaits my magic kiss. I can truly adore the female, but you must have me before you can transform her and yourself. I work my fastest when the male is inspired by love.

They knew more of me in the ancient days and wrote about me in 'fairy stories' where the youths had to demonstrate some aspect of my power in him before he was allowed near the princess. Any loving father would like to see proof of manhood in any male seeking his daughter's hand. They knew of the possibilities of real immortality in those days, for the couple lived happily EVER AFTER.

Now you seem to live in an age that denies all human possibility, while saying that you follow a master who assured you of everlasting life in a transformed world. Why do you do nought to bring about this transformation? Are you Ancient Egyptians who think that life begins with death? In those days consciousness was body centred with the red fire vibration of the earth working upon the womb area of the body to give you the magic knowledge that you possessed in those days, and is symbolized by the bubbling witches' cauldron. Little of me was yet developed in their heads, hence their gods were depicted with bird or animal heads on human bodies. In many of your later cults you have a large mother with a male baby. This baby commemorates the arrival of a new dimension of my powers on earth.

Einstein had a high proportion of me developed in him.

Initiative is my main strength and all males must be initiated into gaining me. In America a survey was carried out on 500 youths that the law had heard of (in trouble with the police), and another 500 that the law had not heard of. Later in life many of the first group were heard of again in some positive field of activity, but none in the second group. Your first duty to youths is to help them gain me, or the more spirited will bash at your creaking static society in order to consolidate me within them. Is it not marvellous that I have arrived on your planet bearing the gifts of Heaven, why do you not affirm me when I am in your young men? Do you appreciate nothing?

Welcome me for I make men effectual, if a man is not effectual he is not worthy of the name of man. I love to demonstrate my arrival upon earth, in earlier times you would have welcomed me with great celebration, now you try to inhibit my joyous exhibition of myself in youths. What is wrong with you, have you died?

Card 2

ENGLISH TITLE:
THE PRIESTESS

ITALIAN TITLE:
LA PAPESSA

I am the Priestess with vast amounts of knowledge lying behind the veil and hidden within my scroll. I sit between the pillars of the Sun and Moon, whose powers can meet at the cross on my breast. The magnetic Moon controls the cycles of my being which all men know only as mystery, because they have not yet penetrated me very deeply. There are no mysteries to those who truly know.

I grow naturally in all girls allowed to display me, and I emanate from all the body to make all their moves entrancing. How I weep for my poor little representatives on earth in these times, for I am everywhere denied with none allowed to take delight in their bodies and joyfully display them. While nudity is illegal I am denied. What muck and mire your filthy attitudes hurl upon me. Where is your innocence, the only state that can keep you with God?

With Cupid's inspiration I course through very young minds promising them many wonders and delights from lovemaking. Then because you do not live in accord with truth they are disappointed when my intuitions are not realized in their loving. Making them think that I was but a childish dream. I am no mere dream. I tell you the truth which would be realized if only you lived according to the harmonies of the cosmos.

I am not invited to council chambers to dance and charm erotically, where I may remind men that God gave them all the Earth to love. My power and wisdom is nowhere sought or allowed. I am walled up in dark chambers of the mind by fear inspired stones of legal statutes. Is there not a knight among you with courage enough to rescue me? Many schools dress my little representatives in clothes like boys, yet send a boy to school in my clothes and he will be persecuted almost unto death. What fear ridden hate you have of me!

I have marvellous magic to give, but who among you knows of it now? Some witch doctors in Africa know a little of my power and 'marry' me while I am in a child, for I can respond to adoration in even the youngest, and through their ritualistic adoration of me, gain a number of powers. 'Lewis Carroll', Dodgson knew how to adore me in the very young and drew from my soul the stories of 'Alice in Wonderland'. These gifts come from the nonpenetration techniques of adoring me. Later at puberty I have other gifts to bestow. The Tantric cult in India knows of some of these, but who else among you truly knows me?

When I truly function in the female she becomes the highest prize the male can possibly imagine, where he sees no price too high for me, nor no risk too great to grasp me. I am the ultimate gift for all that is truly male, with the risk of his life but a minor consideration for the wonders I can bestow. I am truly a matter of life or death to him, and he to me, but there is little I can do but be, until he is ready with the courage and powers that can transform us both.

The key that unlocks me is forged by courage, skill and honour, with adoration as the way to ever more deeply penetrate me. With this combination there are no limits to what I can teach and bestow.

I am all the waters of the earth that seek to be drenched by the Sun. In human form I seek to draw all solar attributes from the male that has gained them, that we may be transformed as the Sun transforms the waters into air (consciousness). I know the dance of the seven veils to lead him ever further on, if he has the power and courage to follow. All true females are priestesses of love. There are seven doors in my vagina, the first, the physical, most any mut can tear, but only those of worth can unlock the six that are psychic (metaphysical), and only then one after another as he gains the power, worth and subtlety to do so. Each one yielding a greater ecstasy than the last until our souls can meet in a supreme super orgasm that will be attended by a vast thunder clap in the skies. Since you lost your receptivity you have forgotten me. Oh men when will you be ready for me? So long have I waited.

ENGLISH TITLE:
THE EMPRESS

ITALIAN TITLE:
L'IMPERATRICE

I am the Empress, queen of nurturing growth. I suckle and feed with the essence of life all living things.

You see by my heart shield that the male has made some impression upon me with his golden phallic wand (see card 4). He has transformed some of my pristine idealism into the warm milk of human kindness and understanding.

Like all female powers I was greater in the past and taught you many things. You tunnelled the earth at my instruction and constructed many imitations of my womb, and held rituals in them that opened you to feed upon my life and magic giving powers. All places of worship then were imitations of my womb where you sought to dance in patterns like those that make life inside it. Many mother churches still have doors that look like my vagina. So much magic is in my womb. The blood in the foetus carries in it immediate healing powers. After birth when the child digests the first suckle the blood chemistry is changed never again to heal as it did in the womb. Once you knew and used such secrets of the blood through me. Much magic then was yours and from the caverns of the earth you came to know the influences of the planets and stars and the tracks their influences made over the surface of the earth. In those days you had the earth mapped out in intersecting lines like a spider's web at the centres of which were particularly strong the different planetary influences. In those days nature guided your way and supplied all your power. Now I am denied and all is artificial.

So much you have forgotten my children, and worst still you have lost your faith. Denying now three quarters of the universe. In past days you were more like me with extraordinary powers of receptivity when you could feel the influences of the planets upon you, and see them psychically without the aid of telescopes. Such aids to vision only became necessary as I was put down in you.

Unlike my daughter I know many of the difficulties attendant to the male. I try to help him and give him succour, often acting as a Temple prostitute or courtesan. No Temple is complete without me for none but I can truly heal the male. He is but a boy and still needs me. My daughter knows what she needs and is interested only in the male who can supply it, but I am more aware of his earthly difficulties, though often I am tempted to possess

5

him and influence him in ways he does not see in order to wield my power. The uninitiated male is never free from my power. Just as well, he would only lose himself if he were. All uninitiated males are my possession living by ways that are a tawdry reflection of matriarchal times. If you would be free of my domination you must have the spirit, or I keep you down where you think you are safe. For on my own I can run the world at a certain level, and best that I do until men are ready to join me. All understanding is mine and all unconscious control I wield. Until you learn the secrets of love I make women want children instead of increasing extensions of their youthful life.

In these times of forgotten femininity I say to my virgin daughters, remember that your virginity is priceless and should be yielded up only to a man of inner worth, for all males leave a psychic impression upon you which can prevent transformative love by a later man of worth. As a virgin you are the priceless prize you know yourself to be, but when that is lost you cannot expect great deeds for your favours. The tragedy of this age is that all my most potentially magical daughters are regarded as prostitutes and turned into them, just because they have much life in their vaginas. Life that could totally absorb the male relieving all his tensions and lift them both to another dimension. But because femininity is outlawed, daughter after daughter is thrown upon the scrap heap. Oh my children, to what squalor your blindness has brought you. In these days of love forgotten, marriage slips away, and pilled up poking goes on apace. It is better than frustration, but no great rewards are here.

Idealistically there should be the gleaming male fused with the enchanting virgin faithful for ever, and your children should aim for this, but be realistic on the way, for legislated idealism has cruelly wrecked the lives of many. Try again to achieve real marriage bearing in mind that it is a long journey to the fusion of two souls, requiring dedicated work on both sides to achieve it. At present practical marriage might be arranged thus: Let the initiated male be married to the virgin with them swearing fidelity for say three to five years with both parties seeking to totally fulfill the other. If at the end of this period he has failed to transform her she will then have the right to train and instruct younger men in the arts of love. This threat should act as a spur to her husband's endeavours. Positive transformations are easy to see, greater youth, understanding, compassion, and abilities of many kinds. The ultimate transformation is a body of a totally different structure which would be immortal.

ENGLISH TITLE:
THE EMPEROR

ITALIAN TITLE:
L'IMPERATORE

I am The Emperor a man partly transformed by woman's love and capable of making just laws and punishments. I carry within me a certain authority. To have me you must know something about something. Theory and opinion forms no part of my real power. You have me by virtue of what you truly know, and this knowledge gives you dominion over certain areas of the earth, either political power or in various fields of knowledge.

Most men when they have achieved some portion of me settle for it and stay where they are. Such limitation is no part of real living, so that their sons and daughters are glad to move away from such stone like stasis. Authority is my being, composed in you of the little you truly have of me, but no man should settle for portions, inflicting only his square little stone upon his family. Life is ever moving and anything static is revolting to those with life. What you have of me will give you earthly wisdom in that area, but no authority to limit or brush aside vast areas you know nothing about. You can be as square as you like, so long as you do not force this shape upon others.

I hold in my right hand the golden phallic symbol of the Sun, in my left the earth upon which a cross appears showing that I have established some authority of knowledge at that spot. You may have seen orbs surrounded by crosses indicating the establishment of many forms of my knowledge in many places. This is the way, as I enter man I give him authority in ever increasing areas.

The little virgin complains of laws I made against loving her. It was not only the fear that men who have little of me have of the female, that brought these laws. It was some brutish men abusing her that brought some of these laws from me. Those who cannot love are not worthy of her. My laws are temporal therefore are do's and don'ts, with me abuse leads to outlawing. I am not a priest who can operate a middle way, testing each aspirant to know his degrees of worthiness in relation to his wants, then allowing or disallowing accordingly.

My function is to establish and administer any knowledge gained from the heavens into the practical lives of men. Before me humanity wandered like cattle to feed. Then, as you may guess, through a particularly successful lovemaking event I entered into man, giving him the first ideas for a feudal system. I started in you as king of a tribal village and evolved to administer empires. I am in fact still your king, but my solitary rule is no longer sufficient for your growing needs. Now I not only need the return of my queen, but an administrator such as a real hierophant to protect the ways of queen and king.

The more observant among you will have noticed that girls in Catholic countries have more femininity alive in them. The Protestants made a great mistake in eliminating all traces of the female in religion. This has led to a terrible deterioration in the creative arts. A helpful first move in the western world would be to have all girls become Catholic and all males Protestant. This could help to solve Ireland's problems also. The Catholic church might then be able to reconcile itself with the body that it hates and fears so much at present.

Since the fall of the civilization based on feminine powers. A power that you now know almost nothing about, and have denied for centuries. I have steadily grown in power and influence in all your thinking. Because of me you still think that family life is the backbone of civilization, it is not, and Jesus tried to show you this but you have not heeded Him. Love one another is the only stabilizing rule, and no civilization will endure which does not practise it!

ENGLISH TITLE:
THE HIEROPHANT

ITALIAN TITLE:
IL PAPA

I am The Hierophant and when I am established in you, you can speak with the controlled voice of God on earth. At my strongest in you I have manifested through your great poets and artists. You will often find their work a mixture of Divine truths and personal idiocyncrasies. It is for you to see which is which.

For many centuries now the earth has known me in only one of my aspects as pope or patriarch. These people using but a portion of my knowledge have done much harm by giving you only the teaching that grows masculine knowledge at the expense of the feminine. This has destroyed your capacity to feel and love, and cut you off from the valuable guide that intuition provides.

In truth I carry knowledge of both male and female powers and their respective forms of consciousness. When one knows of these one knows of the enormous difficulties in reconciling them and becomes aware that if it were not for love they could never be reconciled. Therefore a real hierophant is one who knows the nature of love and many secrets of lovemaking. Love is the principal subject of the hierophant, and as you see card 6 symbolizing my subject stands in front of me.

In earlier times when the female was strong in you, you did not take seriously a place of worship that did not have scenes of lovemaking as part of its decor. Now you have been conditioned to think that lovemaking can have no connection with religion. Do you not think that is a remarkable reversal in human psychology? I suggest you ponder it well to see some of its far reaching ramifications. I can assure you that thinking of lovemaking as the centre of religion is far nearer the truth than imagining that it has nothing to do with it. From hearing my colleagues you will learn that how you are governs what you receive from making love. And the truth of the saying 'I could not love thee n'er so well loved I not honour more' should become clear to you.

As God is Love it is only he or she who knows the nature of Love that can truly pontificate.

There is no church that will let me enter, hence the world has no idea of what God is, nor what is the nature of truth. Poor sheep that you are you never look for yourselves. So that when some ugly power sets itself up saying it speaks for God you look and listen there, ignoring my voice in all the many other places it can be found.

Have you no more courage than to let authority blind you, or follow each other as sheep saying this is the in thing, or it is modern or some other blinding rubbishy remark? I am everywhere and I have little else to say until you have heeded what has been already said.

I am a teacher of what is true, but before I can enter you, you must have humility instead of identifying with what you think you know already. Much of what you think you know has merely been fed into you as into a tape recorder, so that when you hear the unfamiliar your tape automatically rejects it. To provide a true throne for me within you, you must have satisfactorily passed through the tests of the four preceding powers which would give you direct experience of male and female consciousness resulting in the fertilization of both either by magical lovemaking or successful meditation. You must know and equally respect the male and female powers. Then when you are in a state of humility I can enter you to instruct and guide. But any time you lose humility you cut yourself off from my instruction. Humility is the wavelength of my transmission and innocence your means of remaining open to it. When you allow some knowledge to close you your education is at an end. Whenever you feel superior to another person I am no longer with you. If you feel you have qualities another has not, discover how you can give them to him. All this means that you must have a vocation for me. This can come through a sense of responsibility towards the life of this planet you are on, as opposed to being merely concerned with your personal status. You must be willing to both see and hear to possess me. Who among you has the courage for this? How many can even listen?

Love, my subject, is considered not to exist at this time, but you can still find your way to it. Loving begins with allowing, not forcing your state and conditioning upon other persons. Oscar Wilde who often let me through rightly said 'There are three kinds of despots. There is the despot who tyrannizes over the body. There is the despot who tyrannizes over the soul. There is the despot who tyrannizes over the soul and the body alike. The first is called the Prince. The second is called the Pope. The third is called the people.' This is all too true you hold each other in a vile and vicious grip. Just let anyone over twenty gaily dance and skip along the road and see the vile negative attitudes this invokes from the people. What a deadly state you are in. Not allowing joy, to say nothing of loving. You will live in a world where you love one another or there will be no world at all.

From my staff you will see that I have knowledge at all levels. I know what goes on in the world, in the people, in the heavens and in the spirit. Through me you will truly see each other, no deceit is then possible between you. I see the basic alchemy of all persons, and can prepare couples in their respective ways so that they can make magical transformative love between them, just as the four cards preceding me indicate. A knowledge of love is a vital necessity for the next step in your evolution which will come about by a deeper fusion of the two elements that activate you. I have told you how I can enter you, just allow me and I will instruct you. Many priests have affected to possess me, while possessed only by hypocrisy. Those who spoke with my voice were either silenced or thrown out of the church.

If you seek to truly advance you will be tested by adversity to see the strength of your spirit and worthiness. You are to become gods so the powers must test the quality of your courage when you make the assay.

Card 6

I am Cupid who produces the lovers. I am love in the world of human feelings. I shoot my dart where I will and sit back and laugh at the confusion it so often causes in the world of the false values of men. They say that I am blind, but it is they who are blind, knowing not my nature or purpose. When you can see the basic nature of people and their real needs you will understand why I bring people together for reasons that your nonsensical 'logic' cannot see. G. B. Shaw who managed to close his heart in favour of living in his head, never knew me and so said 'Love is a gross exaggeration of the difference between one person and another'. But love is designed to give you a greater identity, and as you can see by my picture, choice is my main function. When I have struck home between a couple they cannot be parted without irreparable suffering. Jesus who knew my nature said 'Those whom God has joined together let no man cast asunder'. Many are in hospital with physical heart trouble because they thought my arrow was but a pin prick. The Ancients knew me better and saw me walking side by side with death. Well they knew that my arrow could bring a couple to life, or kill them if something went wrong. And so it is mort and amour walk side by side. But what are you doing about this fact of life, you slaves of the machines you have created?

While the female has greater dominion over matters of love, her resilience can oft bear its breaks better than the brittle male who likes to pretend he is really above it.

The world loves lovers so long as they don't love too well or inconveniently. Otherwise great jealousy arises, because the people sense that the lovers could transform into something more wonderful than they. What can I do for lovers in this life denying age but kill them? I can only bring life or death. When you do not allow one you must receive the other.

Recapture your youthful imaginations. I oft wafted through your minds as children when you thought of love. In those days you expected great things from me and you were right, but so many of you have allowed a deadly world to contradict my wisdom, and gone through life thinking I was but an illusion. It is your deadly world that is an illusion, not me. I am ever ready to lift you to the heavens when you recognize me. I can put an end to mere existence and bring you life. You cannot tolerate mere existence which you constantly renounce by one war after another.

From my other friends in the Tarot you will learn much about what I need to do my work, but if your feelings and imagination were free I could tell you much myself. Take seriously your sexual fantasies, they are not there for nothing, and as you understand them much will be revealed to you. Your present world is afraid of my instruction. It could not exist in its present form if I were free.

With me coursing through your imagination you would be much more careful about your relationships, knowing that I might strike bending you to the completely unsuitable and causing you irreparable emotional wounds by tearing asunder from them. So few of you know your feeling centre nowadays that you may not understand this at present, but you will. In countries where I have not been completely forgotten, they still know about the importance of virginity for girls and the necessity for effectual men. In their subconscious is my knowledge, disturbing them about the chastity of females, though they know not why. It really only matters where a couple are going to try for magical transformative lovemaking. When the couple achieve the heightened states necessary for transformative effects, both are very vulnerable, and the male in this highly vibrant and open state can actually encounter the psychic imprint of any previous male the girl admitted. The female soul is the essence of impressionability. In heightened states of lovemaking adultery is experienced as an alchemical reality. Chastity is not a moral issue, but a rule one must keep when trying to fuse two souls together. If you wonder why the world has always been casual about the 'wild oats' of the male, it is because no such imprint is made upon him by the female, therefore he is not adulterated. However he is bound by other rules just as strict, which are to make himself, by constant effort more effective and wonderful in every way. Then pass on to the female by making love to her, the benefits gained in his being through his achievements. When this succeeds both are transformed.

If you think love comes with age you know nothing about me. I shoot my dart when I will. It was not for nothing that Shakespeare's Juliet was thirteen in the great romance. As love can transform the body there is some point in the body being young and the imagination open to all possibilities. Also there are certain times in youth when the body is in its most ideal state for the attempt at transformative lovemaking. In girls this is often long before sixteen, so in many countries you have legislated out of existence any possibility of transformative love, in favour of some nonsense you call education.

In lovemaking the female is the body and the male the head. The whole operation is designed to integrate these two. Head growth takes many efforts so the male is often older before he is effective. In real lovemaking the male can pass on to the female the benefits of *all* he has learnt and has done. She does not need to be what you call educated, only really loved. In exchange for this she can bestow fabulous creative imaginative gifts and the holy waters of eternal youth. Do not bother to tell me that older marriages are more stable. They are not marriages merely static liaisons of convenience. You must know about love and abide by its rules before you can really marry.

What makes great loving possible is degree of involvement. How much of all the consciousness of each party is involved, vibrant and stimulated. The honey month now called honeymoon was oft used for this. Where the couple for twenty-seven days, would serve each other in all kinds of loving relieving and intimate ways until their desire for each other became so overwhelming that on the day of consummation the very elements of life that moves them took over and they performed in the very rhythm of the cosmos itself. Love takes time and demands your all. As initiative is so important in a man, the female can often love the successful crook far more than the bank manager. 'Harlots and hunted have pleasures of their own to give the vulgar herd will never understand' – O. Wilde.

The nature of all civilizations are basically controlled by the ruling attitude to love/sex. Therefore if you want a perfect civilization discover the ideal attitude towards me.

ENGLISH TITLE:
THE CHARIOT OF TRUE PROGRESS

ITALIAN TITLE:
IL CARRO

I am The Chariot of true progress. If you have heeded all who have gone before me I am yours for the great journey to perfection. A straight and narrow path is my track leading to precipitous heights before the end is reached. My power and my accomplishment is the use and reconciliation of two opposing forces. You almost never have used my two powers equally in any era, always swinging over to one and denying the other. Then denying the one you were using and affirming its oppposite. So you have never really got anywhere, giving yourselves the impression that round and round is the only way you can go, this is not so. When you use my two powers you will see what true progress can be. Have you the heart for it, or do you wish merely to continue the dreary round of birth, decay and death?

For those among you who 'know that ye are gods' I offer my services. The horses are powered by fire and water. Male and female respectively. Both existing in their own right neither under the domination of the other and both are co-operating and complementing each other. Such an arrangement gives limitless power to all with the wisdom to use it.

On my shoulders you will see the faces of male and female consciousness, divided there as they are in you. My head is created by their fusion. So I can see to my left and my right. Use poetic truth and scientific fact to light the way. I can give and receive, listen and speak. In fact I am in control unlike so many of you who are controlled by the elements you have allowed to grow too strong in you, or limping along because of those you have failed to develop.

There is nothing coercive or legalistic about me. You can only travel my way on your own virtue. If you have to be frightened by law to behave in certain ways you will never ride with me, but continue on your dreary round decaying.

You are on and we are moving when you don't take advantage of anyone you sense to be weaker than you in some way. That is the first sign of real strength. When your will is directed towards correcting your own deficiencies rather than in criticizing those of others, you will know what it is to move. All that you truly see on the journey will take you safely on stage by stage. Be also open to all you hear and judge not the speaker, but see if the words quicken you. The gods play many tricks with us on this journey, putting lies sometimes in professors' mouths and truth in the mouths of children, tramps, we know not who. But the journey stops when you think you know. You do not know until you are perfect at the end of the road.

My straight and narrow path is always between two opposites. To keep going you must avoid what you have always done, swung to one side or the other. For instance innocence and shamelessness about the body and love-making are essential, but you let them lead to casual group copulation. This is not the way, shamelessness must be preserved and so must fidelity. Being able to cope with all opposite things is the way with me. Never either or in anything always both in their season. Emotionalism and objectivity. The natural and the artificial. Abandon and carefulness. Jokes and appreciation. Formal and casual. Receptive and effective.

I am tired of endlessly circling this arena of death, who has the courage to ride me to Life?

ENGLISH TITLE:
JUSTICE

ITALIAN TITLE:
LA GIUSTIZIA

I am Justice when you have moved you will find me. I preside over the balance of all things and my sword falls upon any who too greatly disturb the balance that makes all life possible.

I am a Divine and wonderful creature. On the very rare occasions when men see me truly honoured they can but weep at my beauty. In truth I can give all their true place and role in life, but for this you must love me above all other considerations, and seek never a place which is not truly your right. Concern yourself with not what role you think should be yours, but honour all positive attributes and you will surely find your place.

None escape me, I am never cheated, and those who would ignore me crawl as worms upon the earth. Rise to any height so long as you adore me. I am not law I am justice, greater than all the laws invented by the dreary static world of men. Many law breakers love me more than do law makers, and I help them where I can, though it is hard to give positive help in a world that denies you.

You see I am a beautiful woman, for justice and wisdom lie in the truly feminine soul. Few men are fit to judge because they think of punishment rather than understanding. Why have you denied the female, cutting yourselves off from me and preventing my daughters from functioning in your courts? Have you not seen how the genuine female in her wisdom can often settle transgressions without vicious punishments? Why is she not used in your administration? Are full prisons rather than justice your desire?

Who loves me now, know you not the wrath of woman scorned? What protection do you expect from me denied? How long do you think I shall stay my sword from wiping out the grovelling life denying world of men? When you love me not you see nothing, and you have bound my eyes in the statues over your law courts hoping that I shall not see either, but I see, for I am not in your lifeless statues or statutes. When whilst thou love me and give honour where honour is due, instead of abrogating to yourselves that which another gave? Thou shalt worship me as a Divine light, or never move from where thou art. I who can bless your lives with enlightened joy can also cut you down. When you truly see and worship me I shall transform your lives. Your true wellbeing is dependent on the wellbeing of all others. Any

Jack who thinks he is all right these days is in a serious state of blind idiocy. Live or die is the rule every moment of your lives.

Jesus knew you would not find me in courts of law and wisely advised you to settle your differences before you reached a court. So many times in your courts the guilty are punishing the innocent. Let it be known my wrath knows no bounds in avenging this. For as long as you allow injustice you will grovel hopelessly in the mud seeing no way out of your vale of tears. So few of your laws have authority from God, yet you rely upon them as if they were real. Reliance upon law is no substitute for individual responsibility.

In case you have not seen for yourselves some glaring examples of the guilty judging the innocent:— The trial of Jesus, of Oscar Wilde, or William Reich and most cases of prosecution under 'obscenity' laws, also cases of prosecution involving love 'under age'. Who are you who have no respect for love to say what age it shall occur? And what of those vicious sentences on the train robbers, engendered not by justice but rather by your own greed, fear and envy of their success. For they are by no means the most guilty among you. Then there was that dreadful travesty of me, the Christine Keeler case. You will never live in harmony so long as you allow these dreadful vicious farces to be performed in my name.*

In your present world where there is law there is always injustice. Set to work to put this right before it is too late. In the meantime do not insult me by calling your courts, courts of justice. For they are courts of law and the practice of scapegoatism and little else.

* When performing a play, any local legal injustice can be referred to.

Card 9

ENGLISH TITLE:
WISDOM

ITALIAN TITLE:
L'EREMITA

I am Wisdom, in the first flush of life, I have learned all I can. I am heavily laden with all that I know. In me there are acres of information from which you can draw. I am inwardly excited with all that I have gathered and can instruct you in all subjects up to a point, but my knowledge has made inroads on my vitality.

In the present world I am regarded as the farthest point man can reach. I am often called 'The perfect master' and many people follow me to their death. There is no perfect master unless he be immortal and can teach you how to conquer decay and death in your bodies and souls. So limitation is my most recognizable attribute, and limitation is not life. I arrived here by not taking any chances, moving forward by what I thought was one certainty after another, giving the gods no chance to enlighten me. Such caution is useless to those who wish to live. Prudence petrifies you. Use all I know but do not get stuck here with all the others, imagining there is nothing beyond.

I am the true adviser in all terrestrial matters, but do not expect me to do anything. I am too weary with the search for, and gathering in of information. Take no great step without first asking me, for I can give you information rather than opinion.

Caution has been my undoing allowing me to go no further. I thought the way was made up of certainties, and never moved until I was sure, but life is not like that. The gods demand your all, unconcerned with our reservations, responding only to our will to live and experience all that comes our way. Paul knew something of me when he said 'If you think you are wise become a fool that you may be truly wise'. It means that however much you know or think you know, go into each experience as if for the first time, unweighed down by previous impressions and conclusions. It is not easy that is why I am stuck here identified with what I already know. Still cautiously searching, taking no chances and referring every encounter back to what I experienced in similar circumstances before. So I impose my load on all who meet me instead of allowing new experiences. I try to make other people wise where I should be learning from their 'foolishness' or unfamiliar behaviour. Learn from me whatever you can use, but don't get stuck here. Prudence so blinded me that I need a lamp to see even in daylight. The way of safety leads to nothing but age and death. Jesus was right when He said 'He who could save his life shall lose it'.

Many of you will be like me, have you the courage to let go of all you know and let all kinds of new impressions in? That is what the card in front of me demands. It is the whirl that can initiate you into water if you can let go. I have dithered here for years never finding the nerve to jump into the magic whirl pool. It means being born again of water as you will see by the picture which follows it. I give the illusion of completion but I am only the completion of the first stage.

Never let knowledge keep you from the whirl of life or you will become as Wilde said 'When we are old enough to know better we know nothing at all'. Never retire, life needs your efforts until you drop. Cease all this preparation for death and do something for life. If you do not want to live at least tell your children about the possibilities for the willing.

To pass beyond this point must be your own individual choice. None can be coerced into life, so legislate no force upon those who only wish to die.

ENGLISH TITLE:
THE WHEEL OF FORTUNE

ITALIAN TITLE:
RUOTA DELLA FORTUNA

I am The Wheel of Fortune not many ever play me. Most plump for what they euphemistically call security or settling down.

I am the cycles of life, all the changes you need if you would develop and grow. All the demands that are made upon you, most of which you don't respond to. I am critical to your further progress. If Mr. Wisdom had joined me when he was younger he would not be stuck there now. But he would never do more than he knew, so there he is.

For me to do my magic you must just jump on, take what comes and learn to cope have you the courage? For I answer no questions before you try. I always make demands on some aspect of your being you have not been using and are reluctant to use, but if you respond, on and up you go. Never trying me is never to move on. Some have tried and collapsed through ambition too great for their ability, or because they ignore the signs, others have won an empire.

I promise nothing but expansion, or the sorting of the sheep from the goats. You will not know which you are until you try me. Everything is on its way up or its way down, and in my merry whirl it is still the same, but much more excitingly. I sign no contracts, give you no 'security', but assure you that your life is lost unless you try me.

When you have not advanced you will see my narrow repeating cycles recurring in your life, such as finding yourself in similar circumstances every few years. The periodicity of these repeating patterns differs from person to person, but all matters are governed by my periods of ascending and declining until you take the chance that can break my narrow cycles, and enter my larger ones. Why know me only as a vicious circle when I can be the expanding circle of virtue.

Have you any idea of the vibrant critical nature of life, where the slightest move can make or break? Such is the truth and my confining cycles are often broken by what you think is unlikely. When faced with some problem try extending your arms to shoulder level at your sides and whirl round and round, either to the left or the right for a time. Then consider the problem again. You will find that you have a better view of it, if not the solution.

The human journey to perfection is littered with traps,

riddles and false leads. Wake up, have a go and see the way! It is subtle and yields not to your spell bound behaviour. I wield the sword of death for those who try me in their 'sleep'. Whatever you are doing, do something else. Whatever are your terms and habits of thought, try others totally different. Then you may see the spell you have been in. You see in 'foreigners' behaviour that looks unreal, it is, and your behaviour to them appears as if you were wound up with a key. You're all allowing bits of consciousness to wield you instead of controlling and using it. When you have a piece of consciousness that sees something truly and clearly it is very hard to understand why another does not see it. It is because he has not got that piece, but may well have a piece you don't have and he is wondering why you don't see some other matter.

When you have thoroughly let go in my whirling, your sleeping submerged consciousness can rise again, showing you a world that you did not know existed, and bestowing upon you magical powers. This is what Jesus meant when He spoke of being born again of water, because your sleeping consciousness is activated by the energy form of water. When my colleague (Card 11) The Enchantress rises in you once more, great will be your life!

Card 11

ENGLISH TITLE:
THE ENCHANTRESS

ITALIAN TITLE:
LA FORZA

I am The Enchantress often known as La Force because I am the greatest power on earth. It was my power that built that civilization you all now pretend did not exist. This denial of me comes from your terror, not your intelligence, for you were so pleased with my wondrous powers that you grew me in you out of all balance until I brought the flood upon your heads, because my power is based in the magic dynamic of water. How many of you these days can even imagine a civilization based on a totally different power source? Yet it existed and some of you are now beginning to rediscover its traces.* In all official religious teachings reference to me has been eliminated in favour of solely patriarchal doctrines. Indeed I terrified you and you are still sufferng from the shock.

Since my day you have but superficially grown the Magician in you, and are so captivated by his kind of magic that you can no longer understand my ways. Yet the world is cobwebbed and honeycombed still with traces of the days when you worshipped me. The days when you could charm stones to be as soft as butter and shape them to your will, fly on magic carpets and levitate rocks to great heights. All this and more was yours until you went too far in one direction. Now you go too far in worshipping only the magic of fire so that you are on the point of searing the entire planet. Are you so dim that you can learn only by disaster?

What operates me is that blue dynamic you can see in the sky all around the earth. In the days of Atlantis you knew my secrets and lived upon my powers and all was done by charm. I am still with you, for intellect ever follows the imagination just as the real female leads on the male. But you no longer revere me as in days of old and nowhere now exists for the cultivation of me within you, your imagination. Do you think that rain is old fashioned? Can you even now conceive what a world you would have when you allow both me and the Magician, paying equal homage to us both? We are the two halves of your way to immortality. You see I wear the double ellipse of eternal life upon my head. William Reich was the greatest authority on my powers, in recent times.

I am composed of all the things you have been conditioned to deny or think unimportant in yourselves at

* See 'The View Over Atlantis' by John Michell.

present. Your patronizing attitudes towards dreams and women's intuition. Your thinking that fairy stories are not true. Your not taking imagination as seriously as any other aspect of your being. Your not delighting in and expanding your sexual 'phantasies' and learning that they are not phantasies, but inner guidance to help you find fulfilment. Your not encouraging and learning from the spontaneous dance. All this and more keeps me sleeping and unused within you. Oh how you fear me and set up bastions of 'logic' to keep me down, locked in the dungeons of your bodies and minds. But when I am not free I rot you and drive you to war over differences more illusionary than real. Have you not yet seen that war is just one more of your illusory solutions, settling nothing? My incarceration has brought the emotional plague that now infests the earth. Without me you cannot love. I govern all direct communication and love is the most direct. I carry the secrets of lovemaking that can draw the courageous to ecstasies beyond description. So long as I am denied none can know the great rewards of love. All telepathy is my province as is all what you now call 'extra sensory perception'. Those of you in Spiritualism know that apports are flown through the air by my expanding the molecular structure of the article in order to defeat gravity, and recondensing it where it lands at its destination. Odd fragments of my magic still appear where high sexual activity, water and 'mental imbalance' are found together in one place.

Allow me to grow in you once again. I can save you and give you the power to accurately picture past, present and future. You see by my picture that I once dominated all that was male. I tower over the lion, symbol of masculinity. It was an imbalance then, but not as serious as the imbalance now where the superficial male world has submerged me. I only drowned large numbers of you, he can sear every vestige of life off the planet!

The dynamics of fire and water are behind all you can do. In the old days it was the red fire of the earth that activated my powers like a boiling witches' cauldron. Now it is the superficial yellow fire playing dexterously upon my surface that gives your technology William Reich re-discovered the dynamic that moves me and called it 'Orgone' because I am active in organisms and orgasms. He was 'crucified' like Jesus who also tried to bring me back. 'Orgone' is really the dynamic of water consciousness. To advance you must really know what a thing is rather than having just an arbitrary name for it.

We great powers can only do what you allow. Your free will is sacrosanct. When you let us in we continue to increase, it is our way, and you become spellbound by what we can do for you and forget the other possibilities, but you have always been given great teachings which if you had followed would have kept you balanced instead of falling victims of first one power and then another. You always think you are so clever yet when have you really known anything? Employ us in due season and divinity will be yours. Allow us to control you and you are but fit for the destruction that attends all imbalance.

Please let me save you now, knowing that 'sexual phantasy' as you call it, is the shortest route to where I am.

ENGLISH TITLE:
THE HANGED MAN

ITALIAN TITLE:
L'APPENSO

I am The Hanged Man the sign of truth and most truth is like me, the opposite of what people think it is, so I have always been called wrong and my life threatened by a populace who have not passed through the eleven stages of growth necessary to be able to see.

I am not thinking, I have no opinions, in my state I see or do not see. What I see is how it is. What I do not see still lies further on in my development, but now I know better than to deny that which I don't yet see. H. G. Wells saw some truth and wrote 'The Valley of the

Blind' which very well portrays the difficulties of one who can see among the blind, but when he himself was put to the test, he was as blind as those he ridiculed. For example A. S. Neil (of progressive school fame) sent Wells a report on the findings of William Reich, and Wells dismissed the work with a cursory note. Yet there has breathed no more important man than Reich for many a century. He has as you would expect, been called mad by the 'dead' whose very lifelessness irked him beyond endurance. Through his work the Enchantress who gave me my last great instruction, can be brought out of the dungeons of our minds. For Reich revealed the power dynamic of her fabulous abilities. He called her energy Orgone, but what it really is, is the energy essence from which water is derived, metaphysical water. Some of my colleagues have also told you this, but I make no apology for repeating it because when you see this for yourselves so much religious teaching which you have not under-stood will suddenly become clear to you, and you will be able to advance.

When we live among primitive people almost certain death confronts anyone who sees some truth. You see Death (Card 13) is just in front of me. The savages of his time thrust it upon Reich as they have thrust it upon many before him who dared to tell them something true. Don't bother warring on other countries that you think are less worthy than yours. If you dedicate yourselves to putting your own house in order and succeed, it will not be long before the world follows your example. It is easier to kill other people than to improve yourselves, but it is not the way to happiness.

Handling truth oneself is difficult enough without the wrath of the unawakened. Many have seen some and gone mad, putting their lives in danger if not actually losing them. Truth sits not easily on imbalanced development. If you seek me, and I am to be found, be sure that you can operate in all four elements or my power may destroy you. For balanced growth you must develop and pay equal respect to logical thought, imagination, intuition and psychic phenomena, be manually practical, and be active and have initiative. If you are partisan about any of these functions, thinking any to be more important than another you will not get very far, and if some truth should touch you, you are likely to quail. As you do not know what is truly important let all things instruct you.

What the majority think or do is almost always ipso facto wrong. Just by the fact that the majority are doing it. There should be no such majority. There should be many groups engaged in all manner of different activities and thought patterns, with no over all establishment to say what is important or unimportant.

Individually I am often something you cannot face. Those of you studying certain branches of yoga will know that the practice of standing on your head for say ten minutes a day is a fruitful exercise.

ENGLISH TITLE:
DEATH

ITALIAN TITLE:
NONE

I am Death, here at a critical point on your journey. None pass me without all the answers. Most of you never come to me via the lively search for life, where my performance could be truly dramatic and enlightening for all who wish to see. I am at my best when dramatically cutting down the aspirant who challenges me without the pass word, but who among you now risks himself for life? I grow tired of all this dreary decaying into my arms. I am but a door keeper to prevent the unworthy from entering the realm of the ever living. How bored I become when none of you ever even try. Are you satisfied with your little short life, gone in decay before you have learned how to live? Oh come those who would challenge me, let us fully play the drama of living, begone the drear of mere existing. Close your ranks against me as you close against those you call your enemies. I am your only enemy. You imagine all the others because you have not the courage to challenge me. But together you can defeat me, for I must let the worthy pass.

None grow towards a fit state to challenge me without a dramatic death, thunder, lightning and torn temple raiments. Dr. C. Jung grew and made discoveries which can threaten my domain, so that when he died I rose a thunder storm and split his favourite tree in two by lightning. I love to terrify, it keeps all faint hearts from ever thinking of a challenge, and they imagine all is mine.

Aren't I clever to play the role of the only certain god of your world? Yet if you wished you could blast me off the face of the earth for ever. Instead you call me in again and again as the ultimate solution to all your problems, but I am not, as you will soon discover if you have not discovered already. How I laugh with glee over your devotion to me, as you slaughter each other by the thousands or millions over some silly point of difference which you don't even remember by the time the slaughter's finished. As Dean Swift tried to show you in 'Gulliver's Travels'. And you thought his wisdom was fairy stories!

How long will you put up with my silly grin at all your endeavours? I am sick of controlling your world and would love to be released. Is there neither courage nor vision anywhere among you?

As you advance only by human sacrifice, making your discoveries largely in wars. In the application of these discoveries I always claim more victims. Live as vitally in 'peace' as you do in war and you could well get past me.

I walk side by side with great love, with those who can really love, because love can defeat me and I must be on my guard to nip in and destroy them before the challenge becomes too powerful. It is not for nothing that the great love stories of history end in disaster. These stories should teach you but they don't, because you have destroyed your souls in wars, and it is only the soul that can recognize the truth.

ENGLISH TITLE:
TIME

ITALIAN TITLE:
LA TEMPERANZA

I am Temperance, time, the great alchemist, through me all comes to fruition and every form find its ultimate destiny. I transform that which is base and low to the highest quality it can reach. Work with me and become wonderful. To know me you must see through death. You have not conquered him yet, for the devil is still in front of me (Card 15), doing his best to hold back my work.

My work for you is to improve you in every way until you transform and mutate into perfection and immortality. My work done, I shall fly away, because eternity will then be here. Eternity is timelessness, not endless quantities of me. I am but a local process between you, the sun and the planets and, when my work is done you will live in the timelessness that is in space now. I am no ultimate fact, just an alchemaical process going on in and around you that the ancient alchemists used to try to imitate and speed up in one way or another. You have lost much since you gave up alchemy.

Take me not as a fixed fact, I am but a movement. You will know me better by looking within rather than thinking that I exist as an unalterable fact of your cosmos. Note all the different ways that you experience me. In love I fly, in boredom my feet are lead. In fact whenever you are engaged in matters that enhance life my wings are swift. Note also how the years of your age alter your experience of me. There are many factors and planetary influences at play in these different experiences of me. My work is so vital none of me should be lost. Your very life is dependent on my work, use me every minute.*

As you see by my vessels I am not of a single nature, and if you would know me you must not think of me moving in only one direction.† Backwards and forwards goes the way, as with the life fluid I am mixing. The conscious mind is quite controlled by thinking of the Sun as the touch stone for all time. It can prove it and demonstrate it as a fact. It is the very stuff it lives by and with which it justifies its logic. But this is no fact of the universe, what happens to the basis of his logical mind when you take him far outside the Solar clock? What does he know then. On what premise then stands the basis of his logic? All his great concepts based on some

* See the work of Paracelsus on time.
† See Rodney Collin's work on the nature of time.

mere local phenomenon. Yet with this tiny portion he would rule as king, but not for long I can assure him, for Solar emissions are but half my power, airborne by the intellect. In my other hand I hold the vessel of earth, container of a very different power, water, whose very different time scale was once judged by the movements in the night sky. The more you discover about Atlantis the more you will discover about a forgotten aspect of me. Consider the effects on your idea of time by the world having changed its axis as it did in the past, and ask yourselves did the world once spin in the opposite direction?

I bring the sun and rain of all growth, but at present you will only accept sun from me, so that when anyone tries to bring you the wisdom of water you hiss and spit with fear and derision. I shall correct this in my way, which is time, although your civilization will have to be destroyed before I can do so, because it will not allow the other half of my great process. How you waste me in this age! The devil everywhere blocking me. Will you not allow me to do my work without having to be destroyed by the multi-million first?

When you allow only one half of my powers you are deceived and limit yourselves. Do you not see that I have two fluids to mix, all that operates all things male, and all that operates all things female? One essence operates all that the conscious mind is capable of, the other operates all that your now subconscious mind is capable of. My work is to feed you both of them that you may integrate them and transform yourselves and the world to perfection. But you have drunk so deeply and so long from my yellow solar essence that you have almost completely forgotten the powers, charm and wisdom of my blue water essence. Though in past times you drank only of the blue and built a magical world by it. Ignoring in those days the yellow I was offering, such imbalance brought catastrophe, because since the FALL the world had been shrouded in mists, so that when you developed in yourselves and on the earth the highest degree possible to reach with the blue vibration, metaphysical water touched material water and brought those mists down upon you as the most dreadful deluge. Light and colour then came upon the earth. The rainbow was seen and so was the sun. From that moment you began to feed upon my vessel of fire, patriarchy was born. The terrifying shock that the flood had been, opened the few survivors to receive the first spark of my solar consciousness.

Ever since those days you have drawn an increasing amount of my fire based consciousness into yourselves until now, when at any minute you could convert metaphysical fire into material fire all over the earth covering it with flames as you once covered it with water by a totally different means. Are death and disaster to ever be your only instructors? You experience in every way the results of the elements you are using. Be sure that they are balanced in you. Drink with equal gratitude from the contents of both my vessels whose main attributes are listed below.

In my left hand all female qualities	In my right hand, all male qualities
Water	Fire
Main symbols the moon and woman.	Main symbols the sun and man.
Night relaxation.	Day tension.
The Goddess	God the Father
Rituals designed to heighten all forms of receptivity. Direct perception, touch,	Rituals intended to heighten all aspects of the will, initiative, discipline. To

smell, taste, hearing, insight, precognition. Delight in nude forms 'free love'. Belief in the individual. Spellbinding, imagination, personal magnetism, telepathy, enchantment. Control by women.

encourage efforts, learning, reason and logic. Insistence on clothes. Belief in the organized group. Love rigorously controlled. The block against love is the foundation stone of all patriarchal religions. Control by men.

Allowing these two great powers in you at the appropriate times will further my great work and lead the worthy to perfection. You need not think of this process in terms of your present very limited likes and dislikes. It has little relationship with your present state.

ENGLISH TITLE:
THE DEVIL

ITALIAN TITLE:
IL DIAVOLO

I am The Devil and I rule the world and pass all my servants on to Death. We are the two supreme powers you serve so well. My foundation stone is taboo, composed of all the positive qualities and activities you should allow, but fear and fashion prevent. All the activities that the way of life of your time and country disallow. I am the force which always denies your greater possibilities.

I wield my power through your fear, ignorance,*

* Ignorance does not mean uneducated, it means to take no notice.

stupidity and blindness. Oscar Wilde put his finger on my source of power when he said 'The only sin is stupidity'. It takes many forms and often abounds in the 'clever'. If you dispelled these limitations I would disintegrate and be no more. See, I only need loose collars on my servants, they could easily slip them over their heads and be free, but courage is needed for that. Better the devil you know they say, and stand there in my service.

As I stand in the path of Divine will whose power is love, I draw on that power and become mighty by turning it into hate. And what powers I wield with this, so many groups I bind together by their hatred of other groups, so that if one member should suggest any virtue in another group his companions are likely to kill him. What a stock in trade for me is human fear. I can hold up all true progress with it.

All injustice serves me, sowing the seeds of hate that I know how well to wield. My favourite mask is self-righteousness. In this guise I have done some of my most dastardly deeds. Whenever you see this mask be sure that I am behind it. For it is not possible to love one another and be selfrighteous. Any group that tells you they have got god have invariably got me. To test them is easy, walk in and say you're just out of jail. Walk in in the nude, or drunk, or pepped up on pills. If you receive a negative reaction it is I who am in control. God has never touched them and I am well entrenched.

Jesus knew my nature well, so nought annoyed him more than hypocrites. All hypocrites are in my service and none serve me better than these, because falsity is my way, all that misleads, leads you to me. If you are not true to yourself about yourself you will never be free of me, nor recognize truth when it be offered you. I have such power today you think all is theory or ideas, with no power to see the true from the false.

I can afford to be generous with my secrets, for who among you has the courage not to serve me? No group would tolerate you, for limitation is their watch word and all limits serve me. They are my very foundation, divide and rule, that's me! What piffling muck you are, there's no fun in being your master.

The greatest power known to psychology is the power of the stronghold, and that power is mine. It is the fear that makes you conform to the values of your time and place, and while this is stronger than love, you are bound to me, afraid to give expression to what the herd denies. The stronghold is the pattern of thought and behaviour allowed by any group or country with which you are identified. Its workings were well portrayed in 'The Valley of the Blind'. Yes these are my people, they who deny what they cannot see. In that story the man who could see fell in love with a girl the blind did not fancy, and she loved him. He was her only chance of love, yet in the end she joined with those of the establishment who would never love her, to persuade the man who could see to have those abnormal growths removed from his face, that gave him all those rubbishy ideas about colour and light. Ah yes she was mine, neither her love nor her appreciation of love was strong enough to pass me.

Drop outs seek to be free of me in my establishment guise, but merely form groups of different denial patterns in which I reign again. Many laws are inspired by me, and you serve them as if they were from god. And so long as law is your god rather than warmth of human understanding I am safely enshrined. You poor little people my victory is so easy there's no fun in it.

Such is the fear and hatred of the male force towards

the female force that all what you call magic is ascribed to me. Even when the great magician Jesus did his magic you said he was employing me. What idiots! Magic is life, and I serve death. Religions ever invoke my name to put down rivals.

I shall reign until your total destruction unless you develop individual courage, and is that likely? Ha ha ha none but a fool would challenge me.

ENGLISH TITLE:
THE LIGHTNING STRUCK TOWER

ITALIAN TITLE:
LA TORRE

You see I am The Lightning Struck Tower. I am all the civilizations that you have built and God has destroyed, because they were not in accord with the great plan. I naturally follow the devil because it was his hands of denial that prevented you from building a civilization that allowed all positive expression. That is the only way of life that can endure for ever in a transformed world. So long as you keep the devil you will always have me crashing around you. I am his logical and inevitable companion. I am with you until you design a world where every positive expression of God abounds.

I grow tired of ever being knocked down in order to enlighten you, but so often only stopping you from doing one thing in favour of another. Can't you grow great enough to allow all functions? Then I should be able to be truly built and endure for ever. Use your judgement little, it is miniscule as it is, replace it with experiencing and Grow! Compared with what there is to know you have not even started, yet you presume to judge. A cock crowing on a dung heap is wiser than you. I am so sick of your present minute logic into which you try to put the universe, and if you stick to it much longer your rubbish bound edifice will be smashed. Look up at the stars, see space upon space. Do you think an understanding of all that will fit into what you call your logical forms of thought? You are disgustingly mad and only fit for the fire you worship.

There can be no life without beauty. Is the rubbish of your logic beautiful, poetic, warm or vibrant? No truth can be expressed without poetry. A scientific fact is a piece of tiny dust to be blown away by the next discovery. Yet now you govern your world by these particles of dust called scientific facts so dryly stated. There is no life without water! Be sure God will not tolerate such rubbish for long, because in this mental prison you have created there is no room for God. With such tiny logic you can prove there is no God, no purpose to life, nor any need to culture yourselves.

Stop grovelling in the sand, look again at the stars of space that are seeking to enlighten you in so many ways. Let yourselves be as receptive as the night where every light is seen and received. Cease making your minds like computers and then saying the mind is like a computer. Within you is the potential of becoming gods, why let yourselves be captivated by one piece of magical consciousness after another, each time saying 'This is it'?

I shall continue to be smashed, shocking you out of one spell after another until you can see the validity of all ways and have the courage to use them. Shocking is my function and you often simulate me in your mental homes to try to release people caught in various spells of different forms of consciousness they cannot control. How much consciousness do you control? Mostly I see you controlled by the type of consciousness you have allowed to grow in you, tending more and more to lose touch with consciousness you have denied, and often calling it mad when you see it in another person. The figures you see falling around me are on their way to enlightenment or death from my shock.

You're not a very pretty sight from where I stand, and little you do invokes compassion. Your smallness is so despicable. Afraid of each other instead of loving one another. What in your humanness have you left worth preserving? Living by principles instead of understanding.

When a civilization is on its way out I am first attacked at my roots by increasing crime as a warning that your time is evil. If you do not heed the warning and improve yourselves instead of condemning the crime that you yourselves have produced, then a greater disaster occurs smashing me down from the top.

Should you ever awake you will find that you have been programmed and function in season according to the tape, with women thinking that children are her fulfilment and men proud of their logic and unfeelingness. All this can be changed when the spark that is God in you is allowed to grow to control and manipulate these functions in many different and more exciting ways. All is energy and all can be changed as you begin to find the keys that lock and unlock energy into matter and matter into energy.

I am an aspect of the formative forces* and it is not my pleasure to be smashed, but to achieve the perfect form designed by God.

* See Rudolf Steiner's work on the formative forces.

ENGLISH TITLE:
STAR OF HOPE

ITALIAN TITLE:
LE STELLE

I am the Star of Hope. I am always here to give you another chance when the edifice you have built collapses. Sometimes you see this as an irrevocable tragedy, but where you have more spirit you see it as freeing you from the all too many restrictions and injustices that it had created. We must always go on is the rule of life. Not to wallow in what was lost, or be vilified by others when we crash, all endings are chances of new beginnings. To give up is to die. Life is inexorable and will have its way. Bear this in mind and expect little sympathy or help from fate when you have given up.

I am the great aim, that towards which all functions work to fulfil themselves. And so long as you allow life on your planet I shall be here drawing you towards your true destiny individually and universally.

There is really no such thing as a person not knowing what his true vocation is. When a person is lost, saying he or she does not know what they want, it arises from living in a time that denies much of that person's soul and its potential. The situation is that such a person is living in a time and place that does not allow what he or she has to give. You all have something to give. Look well into yourself and accept all you find there irrespective of the opinions of your time about it. Then you will find the inner spark of life from which you will find direction. Though you must know that like all my life affirming colleagues, I too demand courage, because what you truly are may be subject to persecution in your environment, so you must find the courage and deviousness to fulfil yourself. To do or express what is positive all means are legitimate that do not seek to seriously injure another. You will notice again and again I have always helped and in some way rewarded those who never gave up. Whatever you constantly pursue will yield results. Sometimes in very remarkable and unexpected ways. As I Ching says 'Perseverance furthers'.

If you have heeded my colleagues you will know by now it is designed that you should grow, and you must now have some idea of what this process demands of you and the elements you must encourage in yourself. None of these elements take good shape nor give best results unless you gird them towards some aim. Nothing truly grows without aiming towards some particular objective. Going through the motions and hoping for the best is not enough. Let all that you are doing be directed towards some aim that you have clearly defined. Then the elements in you can combine towards this end. The don't really know attitude will not take you very far, and life in the midst of whatever riches will yield but little joy. Whatever aim you postulate, when it is achieved, find another or meaning will depart from your existence. For rewards you must be ever moving.

If you have fiery airy elements strong in you, you will seek power and status in your job or profession. When you have achieved this, for your inner balance, turn your attention to knowing the humanities. You will have to become humble to know what humanness is. When you know both leadership and humility you will become greater and see your own way to more expansive aims. A Golden Rule is that no one who wants to be a leader should ever be allowed to do so, reluctant leaders are the only ones likely to possess the spark of true concern for the wellbeing of others.

If watery earthy elements are strong in you and you are true to yourself, some form of what they call 'magic' in this dark age will attract you. Magic is a television set to a primitive islander, or the underlying pattern of life shown to a scientifically trapped mind. William Reich began to tap again, after many centuries, the power of these underlying feminine powers of the cosmos. Let your aim then be to learn ever more about them and use them for healing people, restoring the deserts you have created, or altering the ill luck pattern of the life of another. It is all quite easy as you will see when you have rediscovered the secrets. Turning to mathematics, say after learning natural magic will provide you with ever expanding horizons. If all this frightens you by its magnitude, let me say that when you are allowed to be true to yourself and learn in your own way, real learning will go on all your life, and you will be astounded at what you can grasp. It's only modern 'education' that makes learning difficult and distasteful. As you can see by the I Ching and Chinese philosophy generally, the ancient Chinese allowed all nature to constantly and naturally instruct them. Retain your receptivity and allow things in, like a child. Don't close when you think you know, for if you truly knew you would never close. Conditions change by the hour, let them keep you informed. I am Hope and I am here for all who try.

ENGLISH TITLE:
THE MOON QUEEN

ITALIAN TITLE:
LA LUNA

I am The Moon Queen of all the waters and all that which is moved by water. Not so long ago the alchemists drew pictures of me with a line to the head of woman and the Sun with a line to the head of man. But who in this age remembers the sources of influences? Once when you worshipped me too well I gave you the word lunatic. Now all my powers are subterranean in you, and you know not what I do. I still influence you this way and that, but these days you no longer know it's me, I draw you towards this activity or away from that, and all without your knowing it is me. Once you knew and co-operated with my ways. You were more receptive then and felt the heavenly influences imprint their messages upon your souls. Now when you have bother with your subconscious you take it to a soul analyst (psycho-analyst). Indeed I am a fallen queen upon your earth. Only in some parts of Africa and one or two other places in the world are my powers recognized and I give what you call magical powers to a few who know my ways. But since you have shortened Moon day to Monday you have forgotten me.

As I am queen of all water, all waters must respond to me. Your bodies and even your brains are largely water. How do you think you can safely ignore me? Sense again my influence upon you that you may better know your-selves and use all your potential positively. While you blind yourselves and deny me I can but play negative roles, giving you psychosomatic disorders and reducing much of your behaviour to the level of animals. You know not at this time what is animal or what is human behaviour. The book 'African Genisis' will help you to see that much you claim as human, is but animal and when you're saying that certain behaviour is only human it is in fact animal. Only honour in all its forms can lift you into true humanness.

Dear scribe I sent a goddess from me to visit you when you were living in Spain. Some femininity still remains in the atmosphere there so that I can pass down more easily, but you hesitated to touch me, showing that you were as terrified of living as all the other dying mortals around you. You show the way but do you take it your-self?

As you see by my picture, water and creatures of water are my domain and animals are much influenced by me.

That is why so many goddesses had familiars, and why children relate so well to animals, because they have not yet denied me. There is much consciousness you know little of in animals, and you could certainly do with it at present. You will not waste your time learning from them as you did once before in early times by imitating their movements and basing dances on them.

The forts are for my protection, anything as receptive and impressionable as me feels the need of protection. Just look at my inhibited influence on you today. All the laws you've made to seek protection only to cause more outbreaks of violence from the frustration of life they cause. But worst of all look at your armies and the nature of their weapons. Do you think that they protect you? There is little difference between you all, certainly not enough to make it worth while killing even one of you. No country is heaven, nor yet another hell. Recognize me once again and you will perceive each other more truly, seeing that your differences are as minute as the tiny pieces of consciousness you allow yourselves to grow at present. Dean Swift wrote 'Gulliver's Travels' to show you the nonsense of your differences, but you thought it was only a children's story. Such is your level of understanding that which is designed to enlighten you.

Remember I control all cycles of growth, not only in the womb, but all over the earth. When you truly worshipped me you had a womb centered civilization. Now your civilization is entirely head centered. You need both to perform miracles.

My powers give much inner control of your bodies. Don't lightly dismiss stories of witches turning into various animal forms, those stories can instruct you. It is always easier to slip back, to turn something more evolved into something less, but think of using my powers not only to heal the body but to transform it into something more wonderful. All can be done with the courage and will to do it. Groupwise you always get what you want. That is the tragedy of today.

I am much involved in the process of renewing the cells of your bodies, which bio-chemists will tell you are completely replaced every seven years. Should you ask 'Why then does my body age?' The reply is most interesting. They say that during the years of your physical growth the body has a higher rate of inner vibration. This higher energy vibration ensures that the body discharges all its impurities. When the growth process stops the vibration drops, and due to this the body no longer discharges its impurities fast enough. Hence renewing cells are deteriorated by impurities and the ageing process is thus in motion. So you can say that extended youth depends on purification. Purification is a tenet of all major cults. What are you doing about it? As long as your attitudes towards each other are unclean, you have not started.

When using Solar or Lunar consciousness to perceive the world, your experiences of what you are seeing or experiencing are totally different and so are the values. They are two totally different windows on the world, and both equally valid. As some parts of Ancient Greece grew stronger in Solar consciousness they called the people of some of their outlying islands who were still strong in my Lunar consciousness, liars.* This is how one sees the other until Sun and Moon are reconciled within you. Many of you now find it hard to understand the language of the oracles of Ancient Greece, because oracles are performed with my consciousness, and the way they see has been forgotten by you. Anyone today who can

* See 'The White Goddess' by Robert Graves.

become deeply immersed in me in order to give an oracle will be inclined to talk in the same unfamiliar terms.

No longer think that your progress consists of more of what you have already, but rather a remembering of what you have forgotten.

ENGLISH TITLE:
THE SUN KING

ITALIAN TITLE:
IL SOLE

I am the Sun, your father that art in Heaven. Ever since the pharaoh Akenaten sensed me as the giver of many human powers you have learned to serve me with increasing efficiency over the centuries. Nowadays I shine with great brilliance almost day and night. Look at your cities at night. Vast islands of light, the technology for which has come from my consciousness through you. These days you are 'all' so bright you can learn anything, but understand nothing. Understanding is a digestive process done in the dark. If it functions in you, you can go to sleep with a problem and awake with the answer.

You must know by now that whatever codes of values and behaviour are enforced upon the people, so they will grow one kind of consciousness or another. Puritanism, efforts and learning grow me in you. All this can make you very bright, but what can you know of the night sky so long as I shine? On my own in you, you become too bright and quick to understand any matter in depth. I have made you superficially very clever, but look at any part of the earth where I reign alone, it is a desert where no life can grow.

Through worshipping me so exclusively you have now learned through the intelligence of my fire consciousness how to turn the world into a desert. I could have done this without you. My gifts can make you clever, but you must seek elsewhere for wisdom.

These days I find humanity almost exclusively proud of my powers in them, tending to deny so many of their other potentialities, nearly all tests for how much of me they have in them. Look at Mensa's brotherhood bound to my worship. Never likely to produce anything because they deny the imagination which is the source of all forms. On my own I produce nothing. I give life to what the female offers me. Image making is a female function. Everything is born of the female and developed by the male. By worshipping me only as so many 'mistresses' you deny me, and so many wondrous 'children' you are denied. Your present performances are akin to your having placed a plastic globe around the earth preventing me from penetrating it as I should. How long do you think your world would last like this? How long do you think your air would last which I draw out of your waters? Yet this is what you have done to your minds, set me up in them as king, but allowed me no queen upon which to shine that I may bring ever more forth from her. Worship my queen, your imaginations, as you worship me. Then a real person can begin to grow in you.

There are many subjects which you can be either too bright or too dull to grasp. Don't think that imagination is less real than me. When you begin using it again you will find it far more real, and able to see totally what is coming. Logic sees only half way around the earth, my partner (water) encircles it all the time and sees 'illogical' changes of pattern that take me by surprise. A creative imagination is priceless.

You may see by now why woman and humanity generally made such a welcoming fuss at the birth of sons, and often threw away daughters. In earlier times you had had all the feminine powers you could, and were very short of male light and skills. So each son was welcomed as another representative of me on earth with a chance of bringing down some of my powers and skills. Less technical countries today still fuss about sons, though more technical countries have become indifferent about the sex of their children, because they have so much of me, and train both sexes to grow me in them, and as my power waxes you will have noticed, more and more males are being born. Everything female is in short supply!

In my picture you can see the little baby male intelligence triumphantly guiding the great mare, symbol of the great female forces of earth. The child is not doing what you are doing, trying to stamp out the mare. He is intelligibly using her powers to triumphantly ride over the surface of the earth and make it a wonderful place for all. Let me feed again upon the wonders that are female that all may be brought to perfection. On earth all growth looks up to me symbolized by the sunflowers, but do not deny me the intuition and imagination that I must look into.

Have you ever seen in a lush valley shortly after rain, when I have come out and shone into it with all my splendour. Have you not smelled then that smell of life in the making? In you the valley is the vagina, and the penis the emitter of my rays. Let your 'valley' dance in her ways, as the earth dances erotically around me, while you adore her through my power. Insist that the 'valley' be like me, where then the joy?

ENGLISH TITLE:
JUDGEMENT

ITALIAN TITLE:
IL GIUDIZIO

I am Judgement and can only enter you when you have understood and lived by all you have read up to this point. It is most unlikely that any of you possess any fragment of me at this time.

See how lively I am and what life I can give. When you can truly judge you are free. Who among you knows me these days? My point of entry is through ether, that tiny portion of consciousness composed of the integration between fire and water. How many of you have integrated any portion of these dynamics? Are not most of you used in a partisan manner by one or the other of them? And all too frequently not dynamically enough by either. For your 'democratic' world allows nor recognizes no greatness. Sees achievement only in some narrow approved line of activity.

You have seen the stages of development; up to nine, the acquisition of many kinds of knowledge and wisdom, even a little holiness, but death still left unchallenged. Then the possibility of being born again on a higher scale with number 10 in which you allow all masculine knowledge gained to be whirled away in favour of the rising water of the subconscious (The Enchantress) thereby entering a whole new world of experience, seeing some truth and dramatically encountering death, cheating him for the time being to go on and see into the nature of time, how the Devil wields his power, his influence in making you create only partial civilizations which God has always destroyed. Seen also how Hope comes again to your rescue and how to make the best use of her. Become more sensible of the influences of the Moon and The Sun. Remember the quotation 'Unless you be born again of water and the spirit'. To receive me you have to be born again of water by the Enchantress. Now it is the turn of the spirit. Here I am if you will receive me.* If I enter, you will be truly immortal! All your body and mind can I transform. Like all great powers I demand your courage. Have you the courage to accept me? All the old self you knew will be gone, transformed into a new and vibrant being. Others have hesitated here and been lost. Life or death is an immediate yes or no with us. Hesitant humans are not the stuff that gods are made of. So back you go into the earth time after time until you

* Being born again was a constant theme in the writings of D. H. Lawrence.

learn the secrets of immortality and find the courage to accept it. In my picture you see me calling you out of the earth again and again with the hope that each life you experience will bring you closer to me.

Please don't judge, as you are you have no judgement, only points of view, and to make matters worse you have crippled your creative imagination. This prevents you seeing much that would otherwise be clear to you. At the moment the idea of immortality is very difficult for you and your ideas about it and the changes it will bring about has little meaning to you, and your comments about it are usually ludicrous in the extreme. Mostly because you think in terms of what you want or don't want instead of trying to discover the dance of life and keeping in step with it. When you were apes would you have envisaged your human condition as it is now?

Allow yourselves to grow, and you will see the way. But don't now try to reduce everything to your present level of comprehension, and be rude and unpleasant about that which you cannot yet see. Blindness is nothing to be proud of, though tis oft at the root of pride. Hence the saying 'Pride goes before a fall' if you could have seen you would not have fallen. You have made a real stride forward when anyone can tell you *anything* without invoking a negative response from you. All is some aspect of the truth and if you allow it you may find where it fits. Then you will begin to build up the ether within you through which I can enter.

As you may gather the journey to me is one of constantly increasing your identity as an individual person. Freeing yourself from the fashions of thought of the group, country or world opinion of your time. Your society recognizes this process in masculine roles at least. All male adults being given the collective title Mister.

Then an advance in any profession brings title or letters after the name which is the same thing. Then if he makes further advances in any field, some kind of title is bestowed in any country with a trace of the feudal system left. But where individual endeavour is deemed to have reached its height he becomes the John Smith, a person in his own right with no need of supporting titles. You tend to be doing all this subconsciously at present, but it does have real meaning, as with most things you do unconsciously. This applies particularly to your unconscious suppression of almost all female powers. Note that when anyone is poetically describing his impressions of something, listeners invariably assume it to be unreal. This is an insult to the feminine. Masculine consciousness because it is so narrow thinks it is more real, this is rubbish.

See now what is in front of me, you have been preparing yourselves to receive me, now I prepare you to enter a transformed world, are you ready to enter?

ENGLISH TITLE:
THE WORLD

ITALIAN TITLE:
IL MONDO

I am the world. The world in a state of paradise. See me dancing happily in a halo of perfectly blended and balanced elements. No more time now, she has flown away leaving me in a state of eternity, eternal life and eternal light. The present fluorescent arc of the sun's light now encompasses me on all sides. I am totally fecundated and realized by him. All has been allowed to manifest, express itself and achieve perfection. All elements of your being are now fully grown, and their symbols look benignly on at the entrancing scene. In both hands I hold wands, the phallic symbols of the power of the sun. They have penetrated all my being and I hold them now forever. Heaven is on earth. Oh why did it take you so long? Denying possibilities all the way. Denial is the mark of the primitive man. Get rid of it and see that all is possible. Note my number, for if only you will allow all positive things you will transform me by your new way of living in the twenty-first century.

You must know that the true advance of any individual affects light in every sense of the word. As you blend conscious and subconscious powers within you, so you truly grow and perform the great alchemy that time is trying to weave. The arc of light around me is composed of the integration of fire and water, energies, activators of your two divided forms of consciousness. When a person has integrated a significant amount of these two dynamics he has true light. Hence you will see many of your masters depicted with a halo of light around them.

How sad my heart, how neglected my charms, how forgotten the nature of my powers, since you elected the patriarch as god. How he hates, fears and shuns me. Saying that the body does not matter, that me the earth does not matter. What a ridiculous god he makes, acting like a rose he proudly lifts his head saying 'I have nothing to do with that dirty old earth'. Without me the rose, nor the patriarch could not manifest. They all feed upon me yet dishonour me. To develop patriarchal consciousness is very important. It gives precision, decision, purity and formality. All of which are very necessary for many functions, but elected as god he is a demon and a killer of all humanness. Anyone possessed by him is easily recognized. He will say that the body does not matter or the earth does not matter, that the real world is the world of the spirit and so on. Such a point of view can only exist in a hypocrite. The spirit is useless if not brought down to me. 'God gave man all the world to love' you cannot love me by denying me anything. If you have spiritual knowledge bring it to me, practise it in the world that I may be transformed, then all will become increasingly wonderful.

Your physicists have shown you that there is nothing concrete in the universe. That all manifestations are phenomena of energy arrangements. You must know now that all can be changed. This is one of the real truths. So many of your facts are based on the idea of a static universe. There is no such thing. Your present facts are but stepping stones of thought, they are not truths. That great book the I Ching which means books of changes, offers you in its wisdom, not static facts but shows you something of the nature of movement. Movement is what truly is as you will discover when you have the courage to Live.

Love me with all you know and I shall present you with image after image to bring to reality.

I am very concerned just now about a serious division taking place in many of you. Where you perform coitus with only your lower abdomen instead of involving all of yourselves. Your spirit, your mind, all your feelings and imagination. To *make love* you must be completely involved. It is no thing apart, and when you know how to make it you will realize there is no more important endeavour in which you will ever engage. It is the greatest application of yourself and your attributes, and can therefore give you the greatest rewards. The female is naturally interested in lovemaking because it is her chance of receiving more solar power, and left to her intuition, has many wiles to draw from the male all the benefits of his accomplishments. From her he can draw visions of new territories to conquer. When the sun shines upon me he does so with all his might and I glow back in return with all I have. We deny each other nought. Why let your silly little fears destroy your tremendous possibilities? Male and female are our agents designed to transform our respective energies to perfection and fuse them together to create the paradise you see in my picture. Please apply yourselves to the Great Work.

ENGLISH TITLE:
THE FOOL

ITALIAN TITLE:
IL MATTO

I am God known as The FOOL in the world of men. And any who seek to serve me, or give forth even a phrase from me has been, and still is, regarded likewise. It has long been thus with you because of the blindness of your narrow self interest. Not until you see that your true welfare is the welfare of all will you see me as I really am. None exist without some spark of me within them, but what person treats another as if I were in him or her?

You are still wielded by the influences of many of the earlier animal forms through which you passed. You see one of these animal influences attacking me in the picture. The situation is similar to Jesus wandering about in the wilderness making a fool of himself by telling people to love one another and being attacked by the animal in the people who could not stand such a doctrine. Your fight over territory is the animal still at work in you. Your defence of your way of life is again the animal at work. You know that animals are limited specialists insisting on doing the only things they can. Sticking to your way of life instead of learning from different ways is the limited animal specialist again at work. You have selfrighteously wiped out many ways of life whose wisdom you now stand in dire need. The positive side of this behaviour is 'bringing heaven onto earth' in the sense that when a group discovers a new piece of consciousness they want to establishing it on earth by practising its values and teaching it to others. The others are often too dull or fixed in their ways and respond only to being taught by the sword. So have you performed in your sleep, but destruction is not the way to me, but transformation. If you think you have something wonderful or superior use it to transform, not to obliterate. When you meet others with a different magic, pool your knowledge and you will find an even greater knowledge. Do not compete seeking to establish one kind of magic over another. Everything has its uses and meaning, it is for you to discover what that is.

Look up at the night sky, see boundless space upon space, millions of orbs beyond orbs. You cannot really conceive of it, no more can you conceive of me within your present limitations. I created all this, and you can hardly step from one orb to another. But if you are innocent, humble and awake you can know me as the fool. The greatest can also be the last and in this form you can know me. I am not the fiery egotistical gods of the past whose powers you needed for growing some strength of character. I am all and have no need to prove myself, that is your problem.

I am detached from your fray and narrow self interest, thus when I speak through fools 'idiots' or little children I am always a source of irritation to you, ignored or decried, for my wisdom is not in accord with whatever piece of consciousness you have allowed to possess you at any time. Why do I speak through such people? Who else would lend me voice? All others are too busy building up some kind of false front, trying to prove how 'normal' they are, too busy rebelling instead of trying to understand and find a truer way. In other words all are too busy holding onto something other than humility. It is only in states of true innocence and humility that you can be aware of me. In earlier times you allowed many of the mentally 'strange' to wander in your midst. My voice was heard more often then, now you lock them away keeping enlightenment even further from you. Using your idiotic 'judgement' all the time, as if you had any. Suspend it if you would know me, for you know not through whom I shall speak or when, but it is most likely to be through one you have dismissed with your ridiculously blind 'judgement' which is interested only in preserving your status or reputation in your crumbling civilization. Truth and reputation cannot occupy the same bed in any of your existing 'ways of life' which could be more accurately called ways of death.

When I speak through great artists and great art who heeds the revelation? Who speaks of what has been revealed? Mostly you have critics who miss the point and speak only of the quality of the technique. And others who see art as a means of investing their money. So that even these means fail to reach you, because as you are you have not the courage to live up to values beyond those which are established around you. And yet if I manifested more strongly in any man or woman, you would run in terror from him or her. So how do you expect me to reach you more effectively than I do? People never want to hear from me, or receive the enlightenment I give. Don't they even tell you that you would be better paid using your gifts writing amusing or exciting fiction?

Those with truly creative gifts invariably have some great deficiency or dependency. It is this spot in them that keeps them humble allowing me to inspire them, but society is usually shocked and embarrassed by the 'weakness' and punishes the genius for it instead of profiting by his wisdom.

Almost all thought patterns conspire against me these days. But you will carry out my will or perish. My command that you shall reach perfection is absolute and the way inexorable. With me is the fulfilment of all promise, against me is suffering and destruction. I am not vindictive. The matter is governed by the nature of the life giving forces that move you which you must use and transform. If you do not love one another you will never be able to do this. Find out what love one another means, you have no idea of its meaning at present. The command of life is all or nothing at all.

I am the Fool, light and bright, and 'Dullness is the coming of age of seriousness'. Ah, how Oscar Wilde often let me touch him, but those of his time were too interested in what he was doing with his genitals to hear me through him. That was their level. Poor chap, crucified as many before him who dared to lend me voice. See the ball in my picture, learn about me at play . . . recreation. I cannot touch you with your heads down tense and committed to what you think is so important at the time.

People often laugh when they hear something true. It releases some suppression in them.

Real communion between you is not done from the tops of your heads, but from your deeper feelings. The unconscious desire to release these and be in a good state with one another is the reason for all the present drug taking. It is very necessary and you should take kief and mescaline for this purpose. Beware of dangerous habit forming drugs which you take because you cannot cope with the present life without love. But you must find the courage to change laws that are dedicated to destroying your humanness. If you lack the spirit to rid yourselves of evil statutes you need not expect to know me. Laws to protect you from yourselves are not my laws. None come to me save by their own ability to live and cope with life.

I am not male or female I am complete. So when you call me He or Father you do not touch me. It is time you found a pronoun for that which is androgynous or else always use God.

All great secrets of life are ineffably simple, that is why you do not easily find them. Humble seekers are great finders. They would find little of any great value without humility. It says in the Gospels, very truly, that I hide the truth from the clever and reveal it only to the simple. The clever are blinded by the brilliance of solar intelligence in them, preventing them from seeing anything of importance to living.

You must see by now that either you learn what it means to love one another, or you will be destroyed. I suggest that you immediately set up an institute to discover what this means, your survival depends upon it. The growth of the elements in you, like all else, respond to love, so love is the only way. There is no other, live or die accordingly.

Occult and the Unusual in Tandem editions

Horror in Tandem editions

U.F.O.'s in Tandem editions

Fantasy Fiction in Tandem editions

By John Jakes

A warrior's sword against the sorcery of ancient evil

Brak the Barbarian	...	...	...	...	...	25p
Brak the Barbarian – The Sorceress		...	...	...	25p
Brak the Barbarian – The Mark of the Demons	...		...	25p

By Andre Norton

'Rich, brilliant, superbly imaginative and fully adult pure fantasy' *Lin Carter*

Witch World	...	...	...	...	...	25p
Web of the Witch World	...	...	...	...	...	25p
Three Against the Witch World	...	...	...	...	25p
Warlock of the Witch World	...	...	...	...	25p
Sorceress of the Witch World	...	...	...	...	25p
Year of the Unicorn	...	...	...	...	...	25p

By Ursula LeGuin

Hugo and Nebula Award winning writer

Planet of Exile	...	...	...	...	...	25p
Rocannon's World	...	...	...	...	...	25p

By John Norman

The Chronicles of Counter-Earth

Tarnsman of Gor	...	...	...	...	...	30p
Captive of Gor	...	...	...	...	...	40p
Outlaw of Gor	...	...	...	...	...	30p
Priest-Kings of Gor	...	...	...	...	...	40p
Nomads of Gor	...	...	...	...	...	40p
Assassin of Gor	...	...	...	...	...	40p

By Edgar Rice Burroughs

Fantastic adventures in Pellucidar

At the Earth's Core	...	...	...	...	...	30p
Pellucidar	...	...	...	...	...	30p
Tanar of Pellucidar	...	...	...	...	...	35p
Back to the Stone Age	...	...	...	...	...	35p
Land of Terror	...	...	...	...	...	35p
Savage Pellucidar	...	...	...	...	...	35p

Forest Webb
The Snowboys

From deep within the mighty Humboldt Glacier the terror struck. Without warning eight men and one woman were suddenly and bewilderingly confronted with an unknown enemy bringing death and madness to the expedition. They had to escape, but the terror was among them, pursued them, stalked them, killed . . .

40p

Elizabeth Lemarchand
Death of an Old Girl   35p
The Affacombe Affair   35p
Alibi for a Corpse   35p

Three first-class detective stories featuring Chief Detective-Inspector Tom Pollard of Scotland Yard, and sure to appeal to anyone who enjoys Agatha Christie.

'A superbly told tale of blackmail and terror'
Manchester Evening News

'A real genuine police detection story . . . a hundred per cent winner'
Sunday Times

Name ....

Address ....

Titles required...................................

....

....

....

....

....

....

....

- - - - - - - - - - - - - - - -

The publishers hope that you enjoyed this book and invite you to write for the full list of Tandem titles.

If you find any difficulty in obtaining these books from your usual retailer we shall be pleased to supply the titles of your choice upon receipt of your remittance.

Packing and postage charges are as follows:
1 book – 7p per copy, 2-4 books – 5p per copy, 5-8 books – 4p per copy.

WRITE NOW TO:
Universal-Tandem Publishing Co. Ltd.
14 Gloucester Road,
London SW7 4RD